SPEARHEAD

GROSSDEUTSCHLAND
Guderian's Eastern Front Elite

SPEARHEAD

GROSSDEUTSCHLAND
Guderian's Eastern Front Elite

Michael Sharpe and Brian L. Davis

Ian Allan
PUBLISHING

Previous page: German grenadiers riding on their Sd Kfz 250 armoured personnel carriers pause during their advance, August 1942. Note frame aerial on the right-hand vehicle which is a *Funkpanzer* (wireless tank). *All photographs in this book, unless specifically credited otherwise, are from the Brian L. Davis collection*

First published 2001

ISBN 0 7110 2854 0

© Compendium Publishing 2001

Published by Ian Allan Publishing

an imprint of Ian Allan Publishing Ltd, Hersham, Surrey KT12 4RG.
Printed by Ian Allan Printing Ltd, Hersham, Surrey KT12 4RG.

Code: 0111/A2

British Library Cataloguing in Publication Data
A CIP catalogue record for this book is available from the British Library

Glossary

Abteilung	Battalion
Armee	Army
Artillerie	Artillery
Aufklärung	Recce
Ausbildung	Training
Bataillon	Battalion
Begleit	Escort
Einheiten	Units
Ersatz	Replacement
Feldersatz	Field replacement
Flak	AA gun
Geschütz	Gun
Grenadier	Rifleman
Heer	German Army
Infanterie	Infantry
Kampfgruppe	Battle group
Kavallerie	Cavalry
Kompanie	Company
Kraftfahrpark	Maintenance depot
Lehr	Training
Leichte	Light
Luftwaffe	German Air Force
Motorisiert	Motorised
Nachrichten	Signals
Nebelwerfer	Grenade launcher (multi-barrel)
Panzergrenadier	Armd infantry
Panzerjäger	Anti-tank infantry
Pionier	Engineer
Sanität	Medical
Schütze	Rifleman
Schwer	Heavy
Stab	Staff (HQ)
Stamm	Cadre
Stellung	Position/static
Sturmgeschütz	Assault Gun
Truppe	Troop
Versorgungstruppen	Service troops
Wache	Guard
Wehrmacht	German armed forces
Zug	Platoon

Abbreviations

AA	Anti-aircraft
ADC	Aide de camp
Arty	Artillery
Atk	Anti-tank
Bn	Battalion
BR	Brandenburg
Brig	Brigade
Bty	Battery
Col	Column
Coy	Company
Det	Detachment
Engr	Engineer
FB	Führer Begleit (escort), Bn (Bn), R (Regt), B (Brigade), D (Div)
FGD	Führer Grenadier Division
GD	Grossdeutschland
Hy	Heavy
IDGD	Infantry Division Grossdeutschland
IRGD	Infantry Regiment Grossdeutschland
le FH	leichte Feldhaubitze (light field gun)
Lt	Lieutenant; light
Maint	Maintenance
MC	Motorcycle
Mor	Mortar
Mot	Motorised
Mtrel	Materiel
OKW	Oberkommando der Wehrmacht
OKH	Oberkommando des Heeres
Pak	Panzerabwehrkanone (anti-tank gun)
Pl	Platoon
PzBefWag	Panzerbefehls-wagen (armd comd vehicle)
PzGr	Panzergrenadier
PzJr	Panzerjäger
PzKpfw	Panzerkampfwagen tank
QM	Quartermaster
Recce	Reconnaissance
RA	Royal Artillery
RHQ	Regimental HQ
Sect	Section
Sig	Signals
SP	Self-propelled
Tac	Tactical
Tk	Tank
Veh	Vehicle
WH	Wehrmacht Heer

CONTENTS

ORIGINS & HISTORY

Like most elite units, the *Grossdeutschland* (or *Großdeutschland* as it can be written in German) Regiment, Division and later Panzer Corps was born out of other elites, first and foremost the *Wachtruppe* (guard troop) in Berlin, and the German Army's infantry training unit based at Döberitz.

The origins of the Wachtruppe can be traced back to 1919 when groups of ex-servicemen known as the *Freikorps* had been banded together by senior German Army figures to fight the supposed threat of left wing revolution and possible invasion from Poland. An an armed body of this type was raised in Berlin and kept in being until the threat of revolution abated. This body was maintained for ceremonial duties and parades and was known as the Wachregiment Berlin until disbanded in 1921. Subsequently, as part of the army permitted to Weimar Germany, a new unit was raised under the title of Kommando der Wachtruppe (Command of the Guard Troop) and this remained unaltered for the next 13 years.

The Wachtruppe's duties were purely ceremonial. On Sundays, Tuesdays and Thursdays, with a full guard and regimental band, it would march from the barracks at Moabit, passing through the Brandenburg Gate, to rally at the Berlin war memorial. On other days simple guard changing ceremonies took place.

In 1934, after Hitler had come to power, the Kommando der Wachtruppe went through several name changes to Wachtruppe Berlin (Berlin Guard Troop) and was increased in size from seven to eight companies with a headquarters company. In 1937 the name was changed once again to Wachregiment Berlin (Berlin Guard Regiment).

The men for this unit were drawn from the newly expanded Wehrmacht, and later smaller groups were seconded to the guard regiment on half-yearly postings with NCOs being rotated yearly. These men had to be of above average height (nearly all men were six feet tall or over) and after an order was issued by Generaloberst Fritsch, had to be the best drill soldiers of their respective units. Each soldier wore a gothic 'W' on his epaulettes and received an additional 1 Groschen (a silver penny) to his daily pay for the duration of his service.

That same year, the infantry training battalion based at the Wehrmacht Infanterie-Schule at Elsgrund near Döberitz was also expanded to regimental size. This unit, which was responsible for developing many of the infantry tactics of Blitzkrieg, would contributed nearly half of its strength to *Grossdeutschland* upon its formation in 1939. From 1935 to 1939 the Infantry School was commanded by the outstanding WWI veteran Oberst Hans-Valentin Hube, who was a master of infantry tactics and wrote the standard Wehrmacht infantry training manual *Der Infanterist* (The Infantryman). German success in the early part of WWII was founded on his mobile infantry tactics, along with those practised at the Infanterie-

Lehr school in Döberitz, and those for armoured warfare developed by Heinz Guderian and Hermann Hoth at Brandenburg. These techniques, as well as parade ground drill, were practised to perfection for visiting dignitaries, heads of state and leading members of the Nazi Party.

For state visits and conferences the Wachregiment was used as a guard of honour. Their drill was perfected to very high standards and old film footage provides evidence of the precision of the parade ground training that dominated the life of the men of the Wachregiment. Long hours were spent practising arms drill and marching in formation and the unit was regularly seen on Saturday mornings parading to the sound of military marching music.

During 1938, as relations between German, and Poland, Britain and France began to deteriorate rapidly, the infantry-training regiment continued to perfect its combat techniques and the Wachregiment dutifully kept guard outside the offices wherein plans for Germany's expansion were being hatched. In the spring of 1939 German troops marched into Czechoslovakia, and Hitler's demands for territorial concessions from Poland met with rebuff. France and Britain announced their solidarity with the Poles, and in response Hitler ordered the Wehrmacht to flex its muscles. As part of this demonstration on 6 April the Wachregiment Berlin was ordered to reform as a full four-battalion infantry regiment; many of the men came from the guard troop and the others were volunteers from all across Germany.

The potential candidate had to be physically as well as mentally and morally fit (according to how these terms were understood in Nazi Germany). He had to be at least 5 feet 8 inches tall, have no criminal record and, unlike recruits for the Waffen-SS, had to have a good standard of education to serve in what was to be the premier unit of the German Army. To reflect the diversity in the ranks, the name *Grossdeutschland* (Greater Germany) was chosen for the regiment, and officially awarded to it by the town commander of Berlin, Generalleutnant Siefert, at a ceremony at the regimental barracks at Moabit on 14 June.

As Infanterie-Regiment *Grossdeutschland* (IRGD) the unit embarked on a period of reorganisation and training during the summer, training that was to prove invaluable during the Battle of France. A week before the invasion of Poland, the Führer-Begleit-Kommando (Führer Escort Command) was formed from the regiment and was then expanded to battalion strength (Führer-Begleit-Bataillon) separate from IRGD.

At the same time some 98 Wehrmacht divisions were mobilising, in preparation for the coming offensive against Poland. Throughout July and early August 1939 units moved quietly to positions east and west. On 1 September that offensive began, as 37 German divisions blitzed their way into the Polish heartland. IRGD, only recently formed, was still in the process of reorganisation and training and as such was not considered combat ready. Thus, IRGD sat out the first stage of the war. The Führer Escort Battalion, however, was involved in the 29-day campaign.

On 6 September 1939 new orders arrived stating that the IRGD was to prepare with all possible haste for an airborne attack against Poland. However, this operation was cancelled due to the advance of Soviet troops into eastern Poland, which made it unnecessary. On the 17th the unit was re-transferred to Berlin, its period of reorganisation now considered complete.

One of the companies (later expanded to a battalion) was detached and ordered to resume guard duties in the capital. On 21 October the remainder of the unit was transferred by rail to the Grafenwöhr training area south of Bayreuth, where it underwent further training and more reorganisation. By early December IRGD had been moulded into a well-disciplined and tightly controlled unit, and one that was ready for combat.

However, in Europe the fighting had met with a lull; after the surrender of Warsaw on 29 September, all German units in Poland had transferred to the west, in anticipation of an attack by Poland's allies, France and Britain. Between 6 and 11 November IRGD moved into the defensive line, taking up positions around Montbaur and Westerburg held by the XIX Motorised Army Corps, veterans of the recently concluded Polish campaign. Their commander, General der Panzertruppe Heinz Guderian was a brilliant tank leader and influential with Hitler.

Shortly after its transfer IRGD was strengthened by the arrival of two motorised assault engineer battalions, trained and equipped for mine-clearance, demolition and bridging. These were the 43rd Assault Engineer Battalion, with three companies, and Light Bridging Column B. Thus 1939 ended with *Grossdeutschland* having expanded from a two-battalion guard regiment to a fully trained four-battalion infantry regiment, by now under the command of Oberst Stockhausen, and actively preparing for the offensive in the west.

Above: Adolf Hitler inspecting an Honour Company from Wachtruppe Berlin drawn up opposite the Reichs Chancellery in the Wilhelmstrasse, Berlin, 10 January 1936.

SPRING, 1940

During the winter lull that became known as the 'Phony War', German Army units rested and re-equipped. The Panzer units, in particular had been much reduced by the Polish campaign, and the devastatingly effective new tactics of Blitzkrieg needed further refinement.

In the last week of January, *Grossdeutschland* marched out of its Montbaur positions to new positions 100km south-west in the middle Mosel region, overlooking the Ardennes, a heavily wooded and semi-mountainous area of southern Belgium, north of the French Maginot Line, and considered impassable to tanks by British and French commanders. The regimental staff decamped to Zell, to finalise details of the upcoming campaign. The waiting dragged on and February and March passed without incident, but in early April GD gained a 16th company, Assault Gun Battery 640, whose primary weapon was the Sturmgeschütz (StuG) III, one of the early assault guns.

In the run-up to the invasion of Norway and Denmark on 9 April the regiment was put on standby alert, but again there was no counterpunch by the Allied armies, swollen to nearly 150 divisions of French (100), British (11), Belgian (22) and Dutch (10) troops. Denmark fell in a day, and although resistance in Norway continued until June, most of the country was in German control by the middle of April. *Grossdeutschland*, now under the command of Oberst Graf Schwerin, knew its time was about to come.

READY FOR WAR

Below: Before entering the *Ehrenmal*—the memorial to honour the German fallen of the Great War—to lay a wreath, Paul, Prince Regent of Yugoslavia, salutes the Honour Company from Wachregiment Berlin, 2 June 1939. On the right of the Prince Regent is the Commander of the Honour Guard and on his left is Generaloberst Fedor von Bock, Commanding Officer of Army Group 1.

By May 1940 the German Army was again ready to assume the offensive, and had 2.5 million men available for campaigning in the west. Hitler had commanded the western campaign to be fought according to a plan devised by General Manstein chief of staff to General Rundstedt, commanding Army Group A. This plan, a revision of the more conventional original plan suggested by the OKH (German Army HQ) placed great emphasis on German armoured forces and their motorised infantry, artillery and support units, and on the tactics of Blitzkrieg.

BLITZKRIEG

Late in World War I the German Army developed basic tactics that eventually evolved into modern concepts of mobile warfare. Those tactics were created in an attempt to overcome the static trench warfare of the Western Front. Elite Sturmtruppen (Stormtroop) infantry units were created to attack and break through enemy positions using the momentum of speed and surprise. However, in WWI these tactics failed to come to full fruition because of the lack of mobility and support needed in order to continue advancing deep into enemy controlled territory.

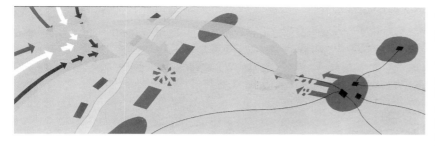

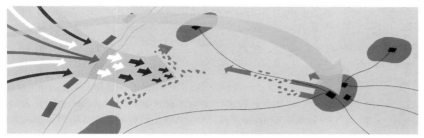

The theory of Blitzkrieg rested on the following principles:

1 Concentrated tank units break through main lines of defence and advance deeper into enemy territory, while following mechanised units pursue and engage defenders preventing them from establishing defensive positions. Infantry continues to engage enemy to misinform and keep enemy forces from withdrawing and establishing effective defence.

2 Infantry and other support units attack enemy flanks in order to link up with other groups to complete the attack and eventually encircle the enemy.

3 Mechanised groups spearhead deeper into the enemy territory outflanking the enemy positions and paralysing the rear preventing withdrawing troops and defenders from establishing effective defensive positions.

4 Main force links up with other units encircling and cutting off the enemy.

During the 1920s British military philosophers Captain Sir Basil Liddell Hart, General J.F.C. Fuller and General G. le Q.Martell further developed tactics of mobile warfare. They all postulated that tanks could not only seize ground by brute strength, but could also be the central factor in a new strategy of warfare. If moved rapidly enough, concentrations of tanks could smash through enemy lines and into the enemy's rear, destroying supplies and artillery positions and decreasing the enemy's will to resist. All of them found tanks to be an ultimate weapon able to penetrate deep into enemy territory while followed by infantry and supported by artillery and air forces.

In the late 1920s and early 1930s, Charles de Gaulle, Hans von Seekt, Heinz Guderian and many others became interested in the concept of mobile warfare and tried to implement it in the organisational structure of their respective armies.

Heinz Guderian organised Germany's tanks or Panzers into self-contained Panzer divisions working with the close support of infantry, motorised infantry, artillery and the air force. From 1933 to 1939 Germany set about mechanising a significant part of its army for the war that Hitler intended to start. In the battle for France, the motorised Infanterie-Regiment *Grossdeutschland* would play a key role.

Grossdeutschland was probably (together with the SS *Leibstandarte Adolf Hitler*) the most powerful motorised infantry unit of the German Army on 10 May 1940. Each infantry platoon had four combat squads and an anti-tank rifle. In addition to the three infantry battalions, the IRGD had a heavy weapons battalion instead of a heavy weapons company, as was normal in standard infantry regiments. This fourth battalion had one light infantry gun company (13th company) with six 75mm infantry guns, an anti-tank company (14th company) with twelve 37mm anti-tank guns, a heavy infantry gun company (15th company) with four 150mm infantry guns, one assault gun company (16th company) with six StuG III (in May 1940 the StuG III was still in its development stage and this company was one of only three German Army units equipped, for combat testing purposes, with this powerful weapon). In addition, the IRGD had received during November of the previous year a motorised assault engineer battalion, 43rd Sturm-Pionier-Abteilung, with three assault companies and one bridge company.

On the eve of the attack, GD was at its start point in the Mosel, and ready for battle.

Left: Small-bore gunnery training at one of the artillery schools.

Opposite page, above: Troops from Wachtruppe Berlin parade for the Commander-in-Chief of the German Army, General der Artillerie Freiherr von Fritsch, Moabit parade ground, Berlin, 5 December 1935.

Opposite page, below: Parade for the Royal Belgian Special Commission to Berlin. Following a wreath-laying ceremony , the Fife and Drum Corps from the Honour Company of Wachtruppe Berlin parade down Unter den Linden, past the *Ehrenmal*, Berlin.

Below: A Guard of Honour from Infantry Regiment *Grossdeutschland* drawn up in front of Anhalter main line railway station, Berlin, present arms for review by the Soviet Foreign Minister Vyacheslav Molotov, the Chairman of the Soviet of People's Commissars of the USSR, prior to his departure for Russia, 12 November 1940. Molotov is seen here accompanied by Field Marshal Wilhelm Keitel (far left), and the German Foreign Minister, Joachim von Ribbentrop.

INFANTRY REGIMENT (MOT) *GROSSDEUTSCHLAND*
as at 10 May 1940

RHQ

Infantry Battalion (mot) I

Bn HQ
- 2 x Lt Telephone Sect
- 4 x Pack Radio Sect
- 2 x Pack Radio Sect

- 3 x Infantry Coys
  Coy HQ and HQ Sect
  - 3 x Inf Platoons
    - HQ Section
    - 4 x Infantry Squads
    - 1 x Mortar Section

- 1 x MG Coy (Mot)
  Coy HQ
  - 3 x MG Platoons
    - HQ Section
    - 2 x MG Sections

- 1 x Mortar Pl
  - HQ Section
  - 3 x Mortar Sections

Signal Platoon (mot)

Platoon HQ
- 4 x Lt Telephone Sects
- 4 x Lt Radio Sects
- 6 x Pack Radio Sects

640th Assault Gun (Sturmgeschütz) Battery

Battery HQ
- 3 x Assault Gun Platoons
  - Each of HQ Sect, Ammo Sect, Gun Sect (2 x Sd Kfz 142)

1 MC Messenger Pl

Platoon HQ
- 5 x Sections

Infantry Battalion (mot) II

Bn HQ
- 2 x Lt Telephone Sect
- 4 x Pack Radio Sect
- 2 x Pack Radio Sect

- 3 x Infantry Coys
  Coy HQ and HQ Sect
  - 3 x Inf Platoons
    - HQ Section
    - 4 x Infantry Squads
    - 1 x Mortar Section

- 1 x MG Coy (Mot)
  Coy HQ
  - 3 x MG Platoons
    - HQ Section
    - 2 x MG Sections

- 1 x Mortar Pl
  - HQ Section
  - 3 x Mortar Sections

Infantry Battalion (mot) III

Bn HQ
- 2 x Lt Telephone Sect
- 4 x Pack Radio Sect
- 2 x Pack Radio Sect

- 3 x Infantry Coys
  Coy HQ and HQ Sect
  - 3 x Inf Platoons
    - HQ Section
    - 4 x Infantry Squads
    - 1 x Mortar Section

- 1 x MG Coy (Mot)
  Coy HQ
  - 3 x MG Platoons
    - HQ Section
    - 2 x MG Sections

- 1 x Mortar Pl
  - HQ Section
  - 3 x Mortar Sections

Infantry Battalion (mot) IV

Bn HQ
- 2 x Lt Telephone Sect
- 4 x Pack Radio Sect
- 2 x Pack Radio Sect

- Lt Inf Gun Coy (mot)
  Coy HQ with HQ Sect and Lt Telephone Sect
  - 3 x Lt Inf Gun Platoons
    - HQ Section
    - 1 x Lt Telephone Sect
    - 1 x Ammo Sect
    - 1 x Gun Sect (2 x 75mm)

- 1 x PzJg Coy (Mot)
  Coy HQ
  - 4 x PzJg Platoons
    - HQ Section
    - 2 x MG Sections

- 1 x Hy Inf Gun Coy (Mot)
  Coy HQ
  - HQ Section
  - 2 x Lt Telephone Sections
  - 2 x Pack Radio Sections

  - 2 x Hy Inf Gun Platoons
    - HQ Section
    - 1 x Lt Telephone Section
    - 1 x Ammo Section
    - 1 x Gun Section (2 x 150mm)

Above right: A camouflaged anti-tank gun, a 50mm Pak (*Panzerabwehrkanone*) 38, manned by troops of Infantry Regiment Grossdeutschland, supporting a assault somewhere on the Eastern Front.

Right: German infantry prepare to jump-off. They are wearing backpacks and carrying support weaponry; the man second from left is carrying a 5cm light mortar.

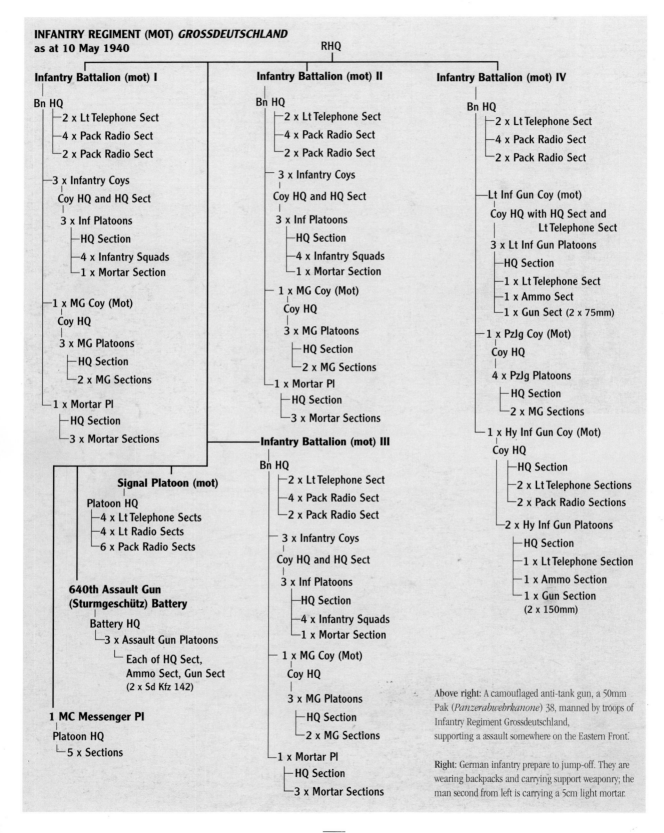

IN ACTION

Above right: An MG 34 heavy-machine gun and crew covering a length of tree-lined country road.

Below right: The German invasion of the west in 1940. *Grossdeutschland* was part of Guderian's XIX Corps in the offensive.

1940: THE WESTERN OFFENSIVE

For the offensive, three army groups, A, B and C, under Rundstedt, Bock and Leeb respectively, were created. The key tank units, including the 5th and 7th Panzers of Hoth's group, the Kleist Armoured Group (with the XIX Corps under Guderian) and the 6th and 8th Panzers under Reinhardt, were attached to Rundstedt's force. It was charged with the most daring element of the plan, a co-ordinated thrust through the ravined and forested Ardennes region behind the main concentration of Allied forces, thus bypassing the formidable French Maginot defensive line. This was to be followed by a race to the undefended Channel coast, before turning to complete the encirclement. In the north, Bock was to make a diversionary attack into Belgium, where the Belgian Army was concentrated on a defensive line on the Albert Canal and Meuse River lines, and seize the strategically important fortress at Eben Emael.

Grossdeutschland was to play a major role in the offensive. Attached to Guderian's XIX Corps, it was to follow close behind the Panzer spearhead and consolidate the German gains.

The assault began on 10 May, with extensive air attacks on the Dutch and Belgian airfields and the seizure of vital river crossings by paratroops at Moerdijk. Bock's 9th Panzer Division then drove into Holland, toward the densely populated 'Fortress Holland' region were the Dutch army had concentrated. In response the French Seventh Army and the British Expeditionary Force (BEF) moved across Belgium to help the Dutch and Belgians. In Belgium, the allied armies soon fell back on a defensive line based on the Dyle River. Holland fell on the 14th, but although it initially appeared that the Allies had succeeded in their central delaying action, Rundstedt had already sprung the trap. Advancing on the central front were Army Group A was opposed by only four light cavalry divisions, the Chasseurs Ardennais, and ten hurriedly prepared infantry divisions, the main blow was delivered by Kleist's two Panzer corps, comprising seven divisions, which pushed through the Ardennes and across the Meuse with almost no losses.

The main body of Infantry Regiment *Grossdeutschland*, supported by artillery and engineers from the 10th Panzer Division, attacked through Luxemburg against the southern Belgian fortifications, while simultaneously elements of GD's 3rd Battalion landed as airborne troops. Rundstedt and his subordinate commanders learned that there was some reason for the French theory that the Ardennes was a difficult barrier for major attacks. It took all the first day to cross the undefended northern portion of Luxemburg, yet on the second day the German forces picked up momentum and neither the Belgian cavalry nor the French Army could do much

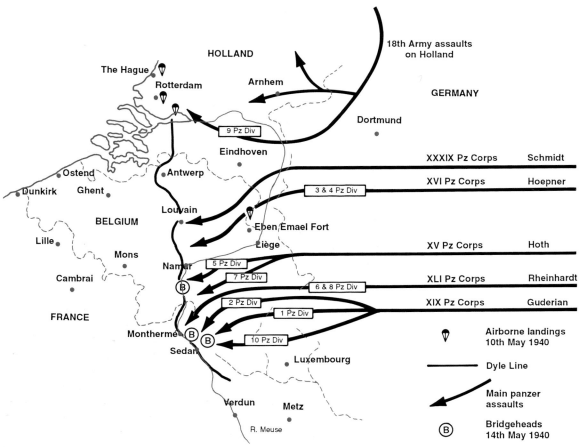

18th Army assaults
on Holland

HOLLAND

The Hague

Rotterdam

Arnhem

GERMANY

Dortmund

9 Pz Div

Eindhoven

XXXIX Pz Corps   Schmidt

Ostend

Antwerp

XVI Pz Corps   Hoepner

Dunkirk   Ghent

3 & 4 Pz Div

Louvain

BELGIUM

Eben Emael Fort

Lille

Liège

XV Pz Corps   Hoth

Mons

Namur

5 Pz Div

7 Pz Div

XLI Pz Corps   Rheinhardt

Cambrai

6 & 8 Pz Div

2 Pz Div

XIX Pz Corps   Guderian

FRANCE

1 Pz Div

Montherme

Sedan

10 Pz Div

Luxembourg

Airborne landings
10th May 1940

Dyle Line

Main panzer
assaults

Verdun   Metz

R. Meuse

Bridgeheads
14th May 1940

Above: Speedy river-crossing was a significant part of Blitzkrieg. The German troops became adept at using inflatable rubber pioneer floats to ensure early bridgeheads when crossing wide rivers.

to stay the advance. By nightfall on the 11th Guderian's tanks had reached Bouillon on the Semois River. It was here on the next day that the regiment had its first taste of battle, skirmishing with Belgian troops whose lines had been overrun. Although a blown bridge temporarily halted the advance, a crossing was forced the next day. Continuing its advance south through Belgium, the regiment approached the Meuse at Sedan via the Forest of Sedan, Fleigneux, St Megnes and Floing, on the north bank of the river.

CROSSING THE MEUSE

In the centre of Army Group A, Guderian and Reinhardt prepared to cross the Meuse on the 13th. Reinhardt's forces at Monthermé and Mézières, and Guderian at Sedan, where the great loop in the Meuse River formed a weak spot in the French defences. In the event, the honour of forcing the first bridgehead went to Erwin Rommel's 7th Panzer Division, which crossed at Dinant at dawn on the 13th. Further south, and despite the fact that neither Guderian nor Reinhardt had built up sizeable forces for an assault crossing, an attack was ordered for the afternoon, in the hope of catching the French before they could prepare. Although the attack, supported by hundreds of aircraft, caused some panic in the French lines (manned mainly by reservists), it proved costly for the Germans. Nearly half the men in the first wave were cut down by French artillery and machine-gun fire. GD assaulted in two parts. The 7th Company to the west of the town and the main body to the east, after looping around the town of Sedan itself.

As the Germans advanced, local French commander General Huntziger launched a hasty cavalry counter-attack against the southern flank of Guderian's thrust, but 2nd Panzer was soon at the Ardennes Canal, where it seized two bridges intact.

After crossing the Meuse, IRGD was placed under the command of the 1st Panzer Division, and advanced south to Cheveuges. South of Cheveuges, the Assault Engineer Battalion split from the main body of the unit and moved west of the uplands overlooking Chémery and Bulson. Moving along the western road into Chémery, it was attacked by French tanks. The main force, having advanced through Bulson, met and held a French armoured attack south of that town.

By now the breakthrough at Sedan had seriously compromised the position of the main allied force in Belgium and, although attempts were made to eliminate the armoured penetration, none of the counter-attacks ordered over the next four days succeeded. As part of the operations to consolidate the bridgeheads over the Meuse IRGD was heavily involved in fighting with the French 55th and 61st Divisions, and 3rd Division around the Stonne highlands, south-east of Artaise, which continued over the next 48 hours. By the 19th the fighting around Bulson had begun to abate as the last tenacious defenders withdrew.

DRIVE TO THE CHANNEL

Moving with impressive speed, Kleist's armour captured St Quentin on 18 May, halfway to the Channel from Sedan, and the next day reached Amiens and Doullens, 40 miles from the coast. On May 20th Abbeville fell, and for all practical purposes the Germans now faced the Channel, having cut the BEF's line of communications with its main base at Cherbourg. On the same day as IRGD began its march towards St Omer, (south of Dunkirk) the British commander, Lord Gort, ordered the BEF to hold a line extending from south of Dunkirk to the vicinity of Arras (the 'canal line'), in an attempt to stop this rush northwards by the German forces. He attempted to drive southwards from Arras, but promised French support failed to materialise and the attack failed, in the face of determined resistance by German units, including IRGD.

Now trapped in a pocket surrounding Dunkirk, its only remaining port, pressed by Army Group A from the south along the fragile canal line and in the east by Army Group B through Belgium, where the Belgians appeared on the brink of collapse, the BEF seemed doomed. As part of Army Group A, IRGD began attacks on the British line south of Dunkirk on 24 May and by the 26th had established bridgeheads over the canal at St Pierre Brouck. That same day, the British government authorised Lord Gort to begin evacuating the BEF from Dunkirk, and the following night the BEF began withdrawing to a shallow perimeter around the port. On the 27th and 28th Wormhoudt and Herzeele were attacked, and while fighting continued south of Dunkirk, the Belgians surrendered. As has been much-debated since, Hitler halted the Panzers and entrusted the destruction of the BEF on the beaches to Goering's Luftwaffe, a decision that is seen by contemporary historians as crucially flawed. the German Army turned south, where the French held a line stretching along the Somme and Aisne rivers. This hastily constructed Weygand Line was badly compromised by the fact that during its advance to the Channel the German forces had captured vital bridgeheads on the Somme. It was to one of these, at Amiens, that the regiment was transferred on 4 June. Here, in the coastal sector, the French had concentrated their main strength, in an effort to prevent the Germans from taking the Channel ports and denying aid from Britain.

Attacks on the Weygand Line by Bock's Army Group B from north-west of Paris began on 5 June. Fighting under the temporary command of the 10th Panzer Division, itself part of Kleist's armoured group, IRGD fought alongside 86th and 69th Infantry Regiments on 6 June through the

Below: The fall of France— *Grossdeutschland* reached Lyon before the Armistice.

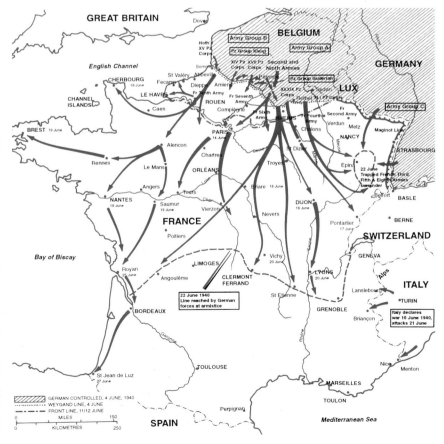

Above: Compiègne Forest, France, 21 June 1940.
French envoys, accompanied by senior German officers
(saluting), walk past German troops to surrender in
the same railway carriage in which the 1918 Armistice
had been signed by the Germans.

villages of St Fuscien and Sains-en-Amiénois, to the south of Amiens, and attacked French positions west of the Bois de Lozières on the following day. While the 1st and 2nd Battalions battled around the Bois de Lozières, the 3rd Battalion advanced to Rossignol, where it rejoined the Assault Engineer Company (which had taken Grattenpache the previous day) for a co-ordinated attack on the French defences to the north-east of the town.

Thus having helped to achieve a decisive breakthrough of the Weygand Line on 8 June, and turn the left flank of the French armies on the Aisne, the regiment began its pursuit of the French forces to the Oise River. Along the Aisne, Rundstedt launched the main attack on the 9th, and despite spirited resistance the French were forced to fall back on the Marne in deference to their open flank. On the next day Guderian's tanks broke through the line at Chalons. Subsequently, Paris was declared an open city and abandoned

IRGD was involved in further heavy fighting south of Amiens until the 10th, when Bock reached the Seine below Paris. With the destruction of the Oise Bridge much of Kleist's group was rushed to the north-east into the area around Guiscard to reinforce Army Group A. Beginning on the 13th, the regiment began a forced march to the Seine above Paris, via Coucy, Villers and Villeneuve. On the 15th, it battled for crossings over the Seine, and continued south in pursuit of the remnants of the retreating French Second and Fourth Armies. On 17 June Guderian's tanks reached the Swiss border, effectively cutting off the 500,000 French troops in the Maginot Line, and France sued for peace.

While the negotiations were underway, IRGD continued to press on south, occupying Lyon in the Rhône valley on the 19th. In and around Lyon the regiment served a month-long tenancy as the occupation force, providing a welcome opportunity for rest and relaxation. On 5 July the regiment marched to Paris and during its brief stay in the capital was reinforced with an additional company, the 17th, equipped as motorcycle troops.

On 26 July the regiment embarked for Colmar and Schlettstadt in the Alsace region, and here undertook training for Operation Seelöwe ('Sealion', the planned invasion of England) until 26 October when this was postponed indefinitely. During this period the regiment underwent much reorganisation. The Heavy Transport Battalion became the 17th and 20th Companies, and at the beginning of September a motorised artillery unit (400. Artillerie-Abteilung) was attached. The next month, a motorised engineer company was added as the 18th Company.

Between the end of October and the new year, the regiment was transferred to a training camp at Le Valdahon, near the Swiss border and here underwent training for Operation Felix—the planned assault on Gibraltar (also cancelled). In November its ranks were further swelled by the addition of a motorised flak company (20th Company).

Infanterie-Regiment *Grossdeutschland* ended 1940 with a reputation hard won on the battlefields of France. It had been involved in many of crucial actions and in them shown the quality of its men and training. The cost was not light. At the start of the western offensive the regiment numbered some 3,900 men and at its conclusion 1,108 of those had become casualties (221 killed, 830 wounded, 57 missing).

Above: Bringing food to his comrades in front-line units, this *Essentrager* (provisions' carrier) is an *Obergefreiter* (Corporal) who has been awarded the Iron Cross 2nd Class. Armed with a rifle he crouches low as he crosses open ground. Strapped to his back is the metal container holding the food.

1941: OPERATION BARBAROSSA

The losses of men and materiel in France were made good during the summer and winter months of 1940–41, during which time there was ample opportunity for new recruits to be trained, and new equipment tested. Although costly, the fighting in France had given *Grossdeutschland* a core of experienced combat veterans whose experience and camaraderie would be vital in the first year of the Russian campaign.

After overwintering at the Le Valdahon training camp on the Swiss border, in the early months of the new year *Grossdeutschland* rotated between the Le Valdahon and the nearby Belfort training camps for a period of intensive training. Unbeknown to all but a few senior officers, this was in preparation for Operation Barbarossa, the invasion of Russia.

As early as June 1940, Hitler had become convinced of the strategic value of an attack on the Soviet Union, firstly as a means of denying Britain a potential ally (and persuading her obstinate people to accept a negotiated peace), secondly as a means of acquiring *Lebensraum*—'living space'—which ostensibly was one of the reasons for the war, and lastly because he was convinced of the Soviet Union's expansionist ambitions in Europe. The OKH began planning for the invasion from that time, and this process gathered increasing impetus as hopes for a swift victory over Britain diminished.

YUGOSLAVIA

In the spring of 1941 Hitler decided to invade Yugoslavia and Greece. The Soviet Union, still Germany's ally at the time, tore up its non-aggression and friendship pacts with those two countries on 5 April and the next day German forces invaded. Beginning on 4 April *Grossdeutschland* was transported by rail from Belfort to Vienna, and from there advanced via Raab, Budapest and Szegedin to Romania. Here it was attached to the XLI Panzer Corps, which was ordered to converge on the Yugoslav capital, Belgrade, from the north-east. The regiment marched into the country on 11 April, via Arad and Temesvar, but met with little resistance from the Yugoslav Army, elements of which it pursued to the vicinity of the Danube River near Pancevo. In the early evening of the 11th an SS lieutenant hoisted the Swastika over the German legation in Belgrade and the next day German armoured spearheads entered the city. Following in their wake, 1st Battalion IRGD, took part in the occupation of the city and from then until the middle of July it acted as security troops in the regions east of the Danube—Weilka, Kikinda and Wertschetz.

RUSSIA

The occupation of Yugoslavia and Greece forced Hitler to revise the original start date of the Russian invasion (15 May), instead scheduling it for end of June. In the middle of May, the regiment received orders to move by rail to the Freudenstadt–Troppau area in south-eastern Germany. Here it remained until 15 June, when further orders came to move to the area south-east of Warsaw, around the town of Zelechów. This would be the start point for the invasion, for which it was attached as a reserve to the Second Panzer Group. Panzer groups had succeeded the highly-successful Panzer corps of the French campaign and were in fact mobile armies, but lingering conservatism among the general staff prevented their being accorded the status of fully-fledged armies. Four of them were available on the eve of the invasion, for which Germany had some 3,050,000 men, plus

Below: A half-tracked 37mm light Flak gun platoon, supported by machine-gun cover, keep a wary eye open for enemy aircraft. In the summer of 1941, following the prophylactic Luftwaffe strikes, there was little Soviet air activity.

Above: PzKpfw IIIs and motorised infantry line up for the march during the early stages of the war in the East.

another 750,000 from Finland and Romania, 3,350 tanks, 7,184 artillery pieces, and 600,000 motor vehicles. These were organised into three Army Groups, North, Centre and South, with support from over 3,000 aircraft. Though all of the German leaders agreed that the war hinged on the use of the Panzer groups, acting independently ahead of the infantry, Hitler was persuaded for the Russian campaign that though the Panzer corps should remain at the spearhead, they were to be in closer co-operation with the infantry in battles of the classic encirclement pattern that aimed at netting the Soviet forces before they could retreat behind the Dnieper.

On 22 June this huge force was unleashed on a 1,800-mile front against the Soviet Union, whose armies were totally unprepared to meet the onslaught. *Grossdeutschland*, marching from Zelechów as part of Bock's Army Group Centre, crossed the border on the 27th/28th in the wake of the Panzers of the 7th Division, and moved toward the objective, Moscow.

Advancing from Bialystock on the 29th, the regiment fought consolidating actions at Slonim against Soviet troops that had been encircled during the rapid advance, and launched another major drive from Baranovichi on 3 July over the northern fringes of the impassable Pripet Marshes towards Minsk. Here another large encirclement yielded more than 150,000 Soviet prisoners. Continuing the drive east, IRGD fought a major engagement at Borisov on the Beresina River, where Napoleon had crossed during his disastrous campaign of 1812. Had the men of *Grossdeutschland* peered down into the water they might have seen the timber supports of the bridges Napoleon's engineers had built. As the regiment advanced deeper into Russia, fighting became more frequent along the route, which took it up to the Dnieper north of Mogilev.

Here IRGD met with the armoured spearhead, and was assigned to the 10th Panzer Division for the assault across the river. After forcing a crossing on 11 July, fighting for the bridgehead continued for the following five days. Having broken out of the bridgehead on the 16th the regiment continued to advance in support of the XLVI Panzer Corps into the area west of Mstislavl near Yelnya, where it attacked

Right: The attack on Russia—the speed of the early advances, the unpreparedness and inferiority of the enemy and the culture of victory fostered by the successes of the early war years all contributed to what seemed like a perfectly executed operation. However, attrition—particularly to NCOs and junior officers—fatigue and, as Napoleon had discovered, the Russian winter held up the Germans sufficiently for the defences to be reorganised. The length of German supply lines, resolute defence and the quality of Russian armour—particularly the T-34—would prove too much for the Wehrmacht in the end.

Russian positions on 21 and 22 July. On 30 July the regiment took part in the attack on the road north toward Dorogobuzh, which met with strong resistance at Ustinova. These battles and other actions at the railroad crossing south of Yelyna, at Vaskovo, raged in summer heat for the last week of July and into August. After more than a month in the front line, the regiment was afforded two days rest in the Dankovo–Vaskovo area from 6 to 8 August, and after moved into defensive positions to hold the salient that had been put into the Soviet line west of Yelnya by the 360-mile-wide advance of Army Group Centre. The capture of Smolensk on 7 August had brought 850,000 Russian captives, and towards the end of the month the ferocious fighting in the vicinity of Vaskovo–Chochlovka–Rudnaya began to slacken off.

The beginning of the campaign in Russia had been characterised by rapid advances as far as the area south of Smolensk, with the fighting sporadic and small scale. Advances across the flat, empty, coverless terrain of central Russia had to be made with the support of artillery and armour and here the regiment's assault gun and artillery units proved invaluable.

On the southern front the fighting had been more intense, and better-prepared Soviet defences had held up the advance of Rundstedt and Kleist. Against the better judgment of his senior staff, who felt the maximum effort should be directed against Moscow, but encouraged by their confident predictions that the war was already won, Hitler decided to send some of Army Group Centre to the south to assist in the actions against Budyonny's West Front at Kiev. On 25 August, the Second Army and the Second Panzer Group turned southward from the Army Group Centre flank. IRGD marched south on 1 September, travelling via Roslavl, Lukaviza, and Starodub. Crossing the Desna River at Novgorod-Severskiy, it was engaged in battles to the north-east of the city to establish a secure bridgehead and, having done so, advanced further south to Glukhov by 8 September. The next day it assaulted across the Seym River at Putivl, but was checked in the bridgehead by strong resistance until the 13th. Pushing on south, the regiment fought at Schilkova, Konotop and Belopoyle, on the north flank of what was now Timoshenko's West Front. The advance was slowed by rain and mud but by the 16th the lead elements of the Second Army and the First Army, which had moved northward from the Dnieper bend, met 150 miles east of Kiev. Kiev fell on the 19th, and seven Soviet armies inside the pocket were captured. In addition to those lost at Uman in the south, this amounted to nearly 1,500,000 men, or half of the current active strength of the Soviet Army.

In the line east of Romny IRGD checked attempts by the Soviets to counter-attack between 26 September and 3 October, and on the 4th began the march back to the Roslavl area, transiting via Konotop and Gomel, and then proceeded on to Karachev, where it bivouacked in positions north of the city on 12 October.

OPERATION *TAIFUN* (TYPHOON)

Ordered by Hitler to recommence the attack on Moscow, Bock had advanced east on 2 October, encircling Bryansk and Vyazma and capturing 663,000 more Soviet prisoners. As the autumn rains set in, slowing the advance to Moscow to a crawl, IRGD was allowed a welcome period of rest and recuperation at Orel on the Oka River. Starting on the 23rd, it marched through the cloying mud to a bivouac area north-east of Mtsensk, in preparation for the following day's attack on strongly fortified Soviet positions in the area. In the last week of October, with temperatures falling ominously, IRGD ground on to Tula, less than 90 miles from Moscow, fighting many actions en route.

To the north-west, German forces were within 40 miles of the Russian capital on 20 October, but their advantage was already running out. Georgi Zhukov had arrived to take charge of the defence of the city, reinforcements were expected from the Far East, and most of the surviving Soviet warplanes were being concentrated around the city. This combination of factors held back the stab at Moscow via Tula on 15 November by Guderian's tank forces in which IRGD played a major role, fighting around Yefremov and Tula.

At the end of the month, an attempt was made to encircle Tula from the north. The regiment assaulted the Soviet defensive lines at Ryazan and Kashira to the east, but was repulsed and lost most the 17th Company (Motorcycle) at Kolodesnya. By 5 December most of the German troops had reached the limit of their endurance, and vehicles were almost inoperative in the severe weather conditions.

On 7 December Zhukov chose his moment to launch a major counter-attack on a 65-mile front against Bock's exhausted Army Group Centre forces. In the lines around Yefremov and Tula, IRGD, now on the defensive, repelled the attacks for two weeks, and then was ordered north again, to the area around Bolkhov north of Orel.

Although his troops were unprepared and poorly equipped to fight through a Russian winter, Hitler refused to allow any retreat, calling instead for fanatical resistance from his men. However, under the weight of the Soviet offensive, the German spearheads north and south of Moscow quickly crumbled, and the offensive expanded until nearly the whole of the Army Group Centre front was aflame. Fighting on the defensive on the Oka River and north of Bolkhov during the last week of the year, IRGD was called on again to reinforce weak points in the line. The regiment was spilt into units and assigned to assist three separate infantry divisions, as Soviet breakthroughs in the north and south threatened the encirclement of the entire Army Group Centre.

Although it had survived, the year has been hard for IRGD. The regiment had fought, and survived, through the extremes of the Russian summer and autumn, and was enduring its winter. Nine hundred of its men had been killed, including many experienced NCOs and enlisted men, and over 3,000 others wounded.

1942: THE FURTHEST EAST

The new year promised a different Soviet Army, one with combat experience, better tanks, guns and planes, and a growing flow of supplies from the US and United Kingdom. Behind the German lines, the partisan forces were becoming a serious threat to the overstretched supply routes, which crossed hundreds of miles of overrun but not conquered territory. During the winter, in Berlin, recriminations for the failure of the Moscow campaign were swift and unflinching. Hitler appointed himself as direct C-in-C of the Army, and 35 leading generals, including all of the Army Group leaders and Guderian and Höppner, were dismissed.

Through early 1942, with men and machines all but immobilised by the weather, IRGD was engaged in small scale fighting on the Oka River between Orel and Belev. Around Gorodok, the regiment fought for ten days to contain an attempted enemy breakthrough launched on 20 January, with the added diversion of partisan action in the forested areas around the town. Fighting to secure the area around Gorodok continued into February, but the regiment was by this time seriously depleted. Already, on 2 February, the 3rd Battalion had been disbanded and its men and equipment used to bolster the remaining battalions. On the 9th, the regiment attacked Verch as part of the operation to clear the Bolkhov–Yagodnaya railroad. Advancing on the north side of the railroad through Novoiginsky, Gorodok, and Fondeyevka, the 1st and 2nd Battalions reached Gorizy on the 15th. Casualties were again heavy, and on the 19th the two remaining Grenadier battalions were reformed into one unit. Another attack followed, this time on Kosovka and Chuchlova, and thereafter the regiment fought consolidating actions in the area while it was reorganised and brought up to strength.

Above right: The *Kettenkrad*, a versatile half-tracked motorcycle, pulling a trailer in the mud of a Russsian autumn. Behind is a Panzerjäger 38(t), a 75mm Pak 40 mounted on a PzKpfw 38(t) chassis.

Below right: The autumn rains swiftly turned the summer dirt and dust into axle-deep cloying mud making most dirt roads almost impassable, reducing movement to 'push and pull' speed.

Above: Soldiers from *Grossdeutschland* probing through the outskirts of a Russian town: another house-to-house clearance awaits.

Below: Hot soup being ladled out from a container into individual mess tins. The men in front-line units took it in turn to collect the rations for themselves and their immediate comrades so as to avoid all the troops leaving their positions at the same time.

INFANTRY DIVISION GROSSDEUTSCHLAND

Between 1 April and 22 May 1942 IRGD underwent wholesale reorganisation and expansion from a regiment into a motorised infantry division. The current *Grossdeutschland* regimental commander, Oberst 'Papa' Hoernlein was promoted to Generalmajor and given command of the new Infanterie-Division (mot) *Grossdeutschland*.

As part of the expansion into a division, new units were assigned to *Grossdeutschland*, which were formed at the Infantry School at Döberitz, Juterborg, and Wandern/Mark Brandenburg during April and May. Underlining its status as an elite unit, new recruits had to conform to exacting physical and mental standards before they could be accepted. The High Command also ordained that *Grossdeutschland* should receive the latest and the best equipment, as it became available.

On 9 April the veterans of the old regiment were relieved and travelled to Orel, and then on the 15th on to Rechitsa on the Dnieper River for a period of rest and refitting. At the beginning of May, the GD Replacement Battalion was reformed as a regiment and transferred from Neuruppin to Cottbus and the following month was expanded again to brigade size. In the last week of May the fresh units to expand GD to a division arrived by truck and rail. Infanterie-Division *Grossdeutschland* (IDGD) was then assigned to XLVIII Panzer Corps, for the summer campaign season. During June the division trained as a unit in the Fatesch area and assembled close to Shchigry for the summer offensive planned for southern Russia.

During the spring Hitler, now in direct and complete control of all operations on the Eastern Front from his headquarters at Rastenburg, outlined his plans for the summer. He ordained that these would be based on a full-scale offensive but only in the south, toward the Don River, Stalingrad and the Caucasus oilfields, the capture of which he saw as the decisive stroke. Hitler's plan was for a series of successive converging attacks; the first phase, in which IDGD would make its combat debut, was to be an enveloping thrust on the Kursk–Voronezh line, which

INFANTRY DIVISION (MOT) *GROSSDEUTSCHLAND*
as at 16 May 1942

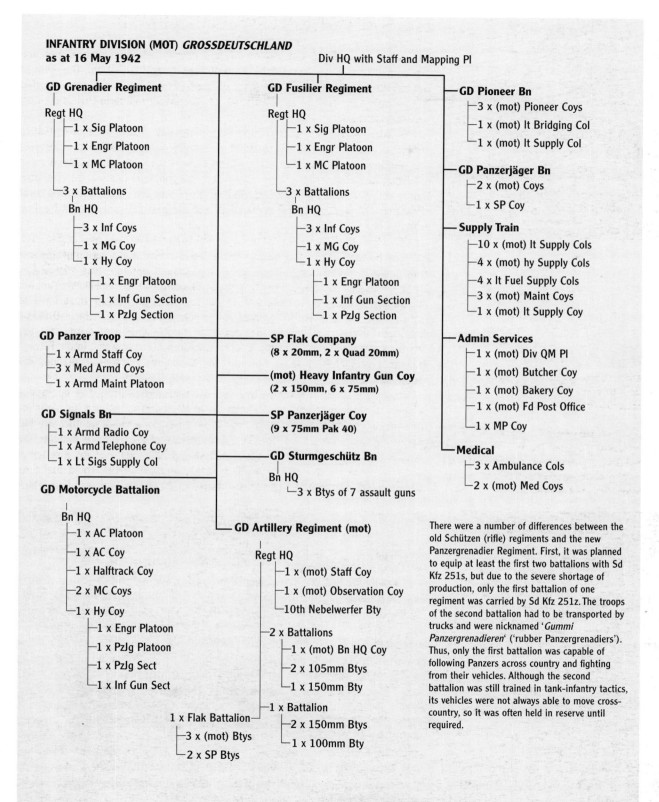

Div HQ with Staff and Mapping Pl

GD Grenadier Regiment

Regt HQ
- 1 x Sig Platoon
- 1 x Engr Platoon
- 1 x MC Platoon

- 3 x Battalions
  - Bn HQ
    - 3 x Inf Coys
    - 1 x MG Coy
    - 1 x Hy Coy
      - 1 x Engr Platoon
      - 1 x Inf Gun Section
      - 1 x PzJg Section

GD Panzer Troop
- 1 x Armd Staff Coy
- 3 x Med Armd Coys
- 1 x Armd Maint Platoon

GD Signals Bn
- 1 x Armd Radio Coy
- 1 x Armd Telephone Coy
- 1 x Lt Sigs Supply Col

GD Motorcycle Battalion

Bn HQ
- 1 x AC Platoon
- 1 x AC Coy
- 1 x Halftrack Coy
- 2 x MC Coys
- 1 x Hy Coy
  - 1 x Engr Platoon
  - 1 x PzJg Platoon
  - 1 x PzJg Sect
  - 1 x Inf Gun Sect

GD Fusilier Regiment

Regt HQ
- 1 x Sig Platoon
- 1 x Engr Platoon
- 1 x MC Platoon

- 3 x Battalions
  - Bn HQ
    - 3 x Inf Coys
    - 1 x MG Coy
    - 1 x Hy Coy
      - 1 x Engr Platoon
      - 1 x Inf Gun Section
      - 1 x PzJg Section

SP Flak Company
(8 x 20mm, 2 x Quad 20mm)

(mot) Heavy Infantry Gun Coy
(2 x 150mm, 6 x 75mm)

SP Panzerjäger Coy
(9 x 75mm Pak 40)

GD Sturmgeschütz Bn

Bn HQ
- 3 x Btys of 7 assault guns

GD Artillery Regiment (mot)

Regt HQ
- 1 x (mot) Staff Coy
- 1 x (mot) Observation Coy
- 10th Nebelwerfer Bty

- 2 x Battalions
  - 1 x (mot) Bn HQ Coy
  - 2 x 105mm Btys
  - 1 x 150mm Bty

- 1 x Battalion
  - 2 x 150mm Btys
  - 1 x 100mm Bty

1 x Flak Battalion
- 3 x (mot) Btys
- 2 x SP Btys

GD Pioneer Bn
- 3 x (mot) Pioneer Coys
- 1 x (mot) lt Bridging Col
- 1 x (mot) lt Supply Col

GD Panzerjäger Bn
- 2 x (mot) Coys
- 1 x SP Coy

Supply Train
- 10 x (mot) lt Supply Cols
- 4 x (mot) hy Supply Cols
- 4 x lt Fuel Supply Cols
- 3 x (mot) Maint Coys
- 1 x (mot) lt Supply Coy

Admin Services
- 1 x (mot) Div QM Pl
- 1 x (mot) Butcher Coy
- 1 x (mot) Bakery Coy
- 1 x (mot) Fd Post Office
- 1 x MP Coy

Medical
- 3 x Ambulance Cols
- 2 x (mot) Med Coys

There were a number of differences between the old Schützen (rifle) regiments and the new Panzergrenadier Regiment. First, it was planned to equip at least the first two battalions with Sd Kfz 251s, but due to the severe shortage of production, only the first battalion of one regiment was carried by Sd Kfz 251z. The troops of the second battalion had to be transported by trucks and were nicknamed '*Gummi Panzergrenadieren*' ('rubber Panzergrenadiers'). Thus, only the first battalion was capable of following Panzers across country and fighting from their vehicles. Although the second battalion was still trained in tank-infantry tactics, its vehicles were not always able to move cross-country, so it was often held in reserve until required.

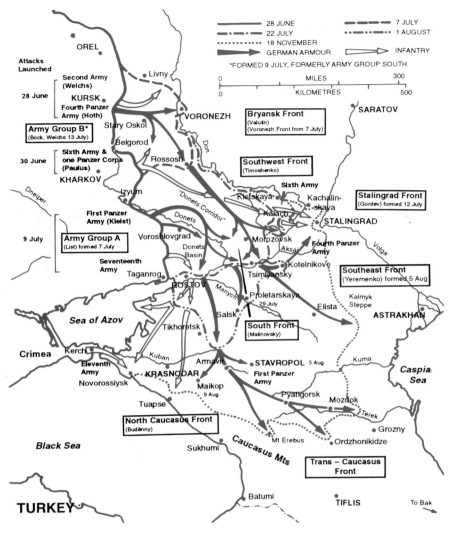

Above: Into the Caucasus—campaigns in the second half of 1942.

would carry the German front to the Don River.

The Soviet High Command, which had also planned to take the initiative when the good weather returned, launched a disastrous attack on the Southwest Front toward Kharkov on 12 May. Although initially successful, it met with strong German resistance and on 25 May the Germans sealed off the pocket and netted 240,000 prisoners. The plans for a Soviet summer offensive during 1942 collapsed at a stroke.

A month later, on 28 June, the Second and Fourth Panzer Armies opened the German summer offensive. Attached to the Fourth Panzer Army, GD advanced east from positions around Shchigry through Russian positions at Ivanovka and moving through Mikhailovka, Paklanovka, and Manssurovo quickly pushed through the inner flanks of the Bryansk and Southwest Fronts. The armoured spearhead reached the upper Don River on the outskirts of Voronezh on 2 July. *Grossdeutschland* assaulted across on the 5th and took the city the next day. After regrouping on the western bank of the Don, IDGD marched south-east on the 8th, across the wide arc of the Don west of Kharkov, to Olchovskii on the Olchovaya.

Although he had originally planned to execute a large encirclement inside the Don bend, on the 13th Hitler ordered Army Group A (to which he attached the Fourth Panzer Army) to turn south, cross the lower Don and force the Soviet forces into a pocket around Rostov. During this advance south encounters with the enemy were limited to light skirmishing near to Tazinskaya and, after an exhausting five-day forced march in the dust and heat of summer, the division reached and crossed the Donets at Mikhailovskii on the 20th. GD then began a rapid advance south across the complex river system east of Rostov, where the Donets, Don, Sal and Manych Rivers meet. Between 21 and 23 July it fought for control of Razdorskaya on the Don. Rostov fell on the 23rd, but its capture did not produce the expected large number of prisoners. Hitler issued a new directive setting forth new objectives, ordering Army Group A to fan out south of Rostov, secure the Black Sea coast and capture the oilfields at Maikop and Grozny. At the same time the army group would have to relinquish all of its artillery and nearly half of the divisions for operations elsewhere.

In the last week of July IDGD battled to consolidate the bridgehead over the Don, which was secured by taking Susatzki. By the 31st it had advanced to the Manych River, and there was relieved. Reassembling at Razhny in early August, the division began transferred by rail to Smolensk on the 16th. In mid-August the Soviets launched major counter-attacks in the Rzhev area, west of Moscow, and GD was ordered to move north to meet the threat. South of Rzhev the division made camp, detailed as army reserve for Ninth Army, until 9 September. The next day it was plunged into one of the most savage battles yet fought on the Eastern Front, meeting a Soviet advance south of the Rzhev railroad at Ssuchtino, Tschermassovo, Vekschino and Michoyevo, which dragged on into early October at heavy cost.

Above: Panzers and Panzergrenadiers hard on the heels of the retreating enemy, 27 August 1942.

On 1 October the divisional infantry regiments were renamed, in accordance with the restructuring program detailed above. The 1st Regiment became Grenadier-Regiment *Grossdeutschland* and the 2nd became Füsilier-Regiment *Grossdeutschland*. (See organisation table on page 29.)

After the bitter fighting south of Rzhev, the division was relieved on 9 October and transferred to the rest area around Olenino. Here it stayed until 25 November, during which time a ski battalion was organised for the division.

During the summer of 1942 the Red Army carried through a reorganisation of its command system, and built up overwhelming strength. On 19 November the Russians launched their second winter offensive, which aimed primarily at relieving the siege at Stalingrad. Attacking north and south of the city, they encircled the German Sixth Army and half of the Fourth Panzer Army.

While the main actions of the winter were fought in the south, bitter fighting also ensued on the northern sector. Attacks on the German Ninth Army, which was stretched over a 60-mile front from Rzhev to Byeloy west of Moscow, resumed in late November. In the sector held by Grenadier-Regiment GD, in the Lutschessa Valley, the Soviet 185th Division attacked in force south of Griva on 27 November, and made major inroads via Karskaya and Gontscharova. South of Byeloy, the Füsilier-Regiment GD (Kampfgruppe *Kassnitz*) met and held the left flank of the Soviet 35th Tank Brigade where it broke through the line at Turovo.

In the centre and on the right flank the Soviets broke through at Dubrovka and Demechi, and the regiment suffered heavy casualties trying to contain the advance. In the Lutschessa Valley, fierce fighting continued throughout the first week of December, as the German XXIII Army Corps battled to contain the Soviet drive. By the middle of the month, the battle had begun to ease and the front stabilised.

Regrouping its scattered units, the GD staff was able to count the very heavy cost of the fighting. Rushed in to stop up the breach by the High Command, which had begun to have unrealistic expectations of *Grossdeutschland's* capabilities, the division had been almost decimated. The lull in fighting was thus something of a blessing, but it was only a brief respite. On 21 December a counter-attack was mounted with the 12th Panzer, followed by another on the 30th.

During 1942 *Grossdeutschland* lost some 10,000–12,000 of its soldiers, and twice, during February and December, came close to collapse. All that remained of the proud unit was a hard core of veterans, and the knowledge that yet more was to come.

1943: THE LONG RETREAT

During the winter of 1942–43 the tide of the war began to turn against Germany, which now found itself contending on all fronts with an enemy better led, well supplied and with a vastly greater capacity to replace losses of men and materiel. Increasingly, the German Army on the Eastern Front was engaged in defensive action, and *Grossdeutschland* was time and again called on to reinforce weak points in the German lines. Furthermore, by now the best Russian aircraft and tanks had achieved a parity with German equipment, which in the coming battles would test the German forces to the limit.

On 14 January, with nearly 300,000 Germans still trapped in the Stalingrad pocket, the Russians moved up the Don for the second time, this time to strike the Hungarian Second Army. The Hungarians soon collapsed, opening a 200-mile front between Voronezh and Lugansk (Voroshilovgrad). They then turned southwards to the Donets, threatening to envelop the remnants of Army Group B and Army Group Don, which was still battling to keep open Army Group A's lifeline to the west at Rostov.

Having stabilised the front at Rzhev, GD marched south to Smolensk, from where, on 17 January, it travelled by rail to the Volchansk area between Byelgorod and Kharkov. At this time the motorcycle units were reorganised as the Aufklärungs-Abteilung (Reconnaissance Group), and IV. Artillerie-Abteilung *Grossdeutschland* was formed at Guben in Germany.

Between 21 January and 8 February, GD fought in the Volchansk battles between the Oskol and the upper Donets River east of Byelgorod. On 25 January the Russians struck northward once more to hit the German Second Army, which was already withdrawing from Voronezh, and in three days encircled two of its three corps. Holding positions to the north and south of Volchansk respectively, the Füsilier-Regiment (Kampfgruppe *Kassnitz*) and Grenadier-Regiment (Kampfgruppe *Platen*) struggled to contain the Soviet advance but were slowly pushed back. On 3 February the lead elements of Kampfgruppe *Pohlmann* of the Führer Escort Battalion were returned to the division, and engaged at Ssurkovo north-east of Volchansk.

Stalingrad was taken by the Russians on 2 February, and Byelgorod on the 8th.

As the Soviet offensive gathered pace, the right flank of Army Group B was forced to withdraw. Between 9 and 14 February GD was involved in the fighting along the Byelgorod–Kharkov railroad, one of the vital communications links to Army Group Don and Army Group A. After the evacuation of Kharkov on the 15th, a 100-mile gap opened between the right flank of Army Group B and Army Group Don, through which Soviet units struck southward and westward across the Donets,

Above right: Wearing snow camouflage coveralls, German infantry shelter beside snow-covered trees and observe a Soviet tank burning in the middle distance.

Below right: In the metre-deep snow which makes the forests in the East almost impenetrable during the winter months, skis and snowshoes were essential but in short supply.

Opposite page, above: Wearing improvised snow camouflage, *Grossdeutschland* troops trudge through snow-covered countryside during an exercise. The lead man is carrying an MG 34 in its light—ie on a bipod—role.

Opposite page, below: A three-man machine-gun crew using the MG 34 in its heavy role on a tripod.

Above: The *Raupenschlepper Ost* (the eastern caterpillar tractor) towing 10.5mm le FH 18/40 light field howitzers to a new position. These tractors proved very useful vehicles that could overcome almost any difficult terrain and obstacle.

Left: Wearing winter camouflage, a telephone wire patrol with messenger dog carefully checks the wires.

moving to cut the remaining communications lines. Between the 16th and 23rd, GD fought to keep the Kharkov–Poltava line open. However, to the south the Donetsk railroad was cut and on the 19th the Soviets had reached the Sinelnikovo railroad junction 20 miles east-south-east of Dneperopetrovsk.

On 24 February GD was relieved and travelled to a rest area some 18 miles west of Poltava. Here it was rested and re-equipped. The newly formed 4th Artillery Battalion arrived, and so, too, the first detachment of Tiger I tanks. In the meantime, General Manstein had initiated moves to close the gap in the German line, and made preparations for a counter-attack against Kharkov, despite the inherent risks of advancing in the spring thaw. GD marched to its starting point for the attack on 5 March, and from the 7th fought through knee-deep cloying mud toward Bogodukov, which fell four days later. The Fourth Panzer Army reached Kharkov on the 11th, trapping several Soviet divisions. After mopping up these divisions, the army took its advance 30 miles farther north and took Byelgorod, and thus regained the line of the Donets to that point. GD, which helped capture Tomarovka to the north of Kharkov on the 19th, was relieved on the 23rd and transferred back to the rest area near Poltava, where further reinforcement arrived in the form of new infantry fighting vehicles (which were in constant short supply). From March to June the division was held in reserve.

In the past two years, the coming of spring had heralded new German triumphs, but although the victory on the Donets that had ended the long winter retreat had done much to restore German morale, no German commander believed that the next summer would see significant gains.

The late spring of 1943 on the Eastern Front was quiet, affording *Grossdeutschland* time for welcome rest. On 25 April, elements of the division were transferred to the Akhtyrka area on the Vorskla River; at the beginning of May III. Abteilung, Panzer-Regiment *Grossdeutschland* was raised at Paderborn in Germany and equipped with Tiger tanks.

Below: An ingenious improvised boiler, complete with smoking chimney, enables the crew members of this Panzer III to do a spot of laundering in hot water.

DEVELOPMENT OF THE PANZERGRENADIER

From their inception, motorised infantry were a key element in the concept of armoured mobile warfare. They were required not only to accompany the Panzers over difficult terrain into action, but also provide both supportive fire power and safety against enemy infantry and anti-tank units while moving under the cover of purposed designed Schützen-Panzerwagen (SPW or riflemen's armoured vehicles).

The first experimental Panzer division was founded in 1934, and included a Schützen-Brigade (rifle brigade), one leichte Schützen-Regiment (light rifle regiment) and one Kradeschützen-Battaillon (motorcycle rifle battalion) These motorised infantry units were tasked with supporting the two Panzer regiments within the Panzer division. Transportation was by both lorry and motorcycle, partly because the Wehrmacht did not have suitable armoured transport vehicles at that time.

Independent motorised infantry units came into being in 1937, when four Infanterie-Divisions (mot) were reorganised from standard Infanterie-Divisions. The second expansion of motorised infantry divisions took place after the French campaign. At that time eight motorised infantry divisions were formed, two of them later reorganised as Panzer divisions. Other motorised infantry units came from the elite troops of both Heer and Waffen-SS, namely Infanterie-Division (mot) *Grossdeutschland*, and SS-Divisions (mot) *Leibstandarte Adolf Hitler, Das Reich, Totenkopf* and *Wiking* during 1941–42. All of these were reorganised as Panzergrenadier divisions in late 1942 and finally became Panzer divisions in late 1943.

The fighting in North Africa and Russia took a heavy toll on the motorised infantry divisions and Panzer divisions, and they were rebuilt in 1943. In June most of the motorised infantry divisions were renamed as Panzergrenadier divisions and reorganised as Type 43 Panzergrenadier divisions in September. During 1943–44 several Panzergrenadier divisions were raised by the Waffen-SS and the Luftwaffe also raised its own Panzergrenadier division.

In late 1944 Panzer-Brigades were created to try to stem the collapse of the Russian Front; these were also occasionally known as Panzer-Grenadier-Brigades. In fact they were a combination of both Panzer and Panzergrenadier arms under the same command, and became the model of the Type 45 Panzer-Division created (theoretically at least) in the last period of war.

The Panzergrenadier divisions underwent final re-organisation in 1945 when units of Panzer-Division *Grossdeutschland* were expanded into four Panzergrenadier divisions. In reality, these were divisions in name only and could be more accurately be described as Kampfgruppen (battle groups).

Although it pioneered the concept of infantry mobile warfare, the German Army was never able to complete fully the formation of Panzergrenadier units, because it was unable to produce enough armoured transport to equip even a fair proportion of the Panzergrenadier units.

Below: Panzergrenadiers on the move. The vast distances, the heat and the dust made movement during the summer months almost, but not quite, as difficult to survive and fight as during the mud-caked autumn and the frozen winter months.

Above: A pause in the fighting in the Caucasus: a PzKpfw III crew takes a short break having replenished ammunition, food and water.

Below: The plan for Operation *Zitadelle*—to chop off the Russian salient at Kursk in a characteristic double pincer.

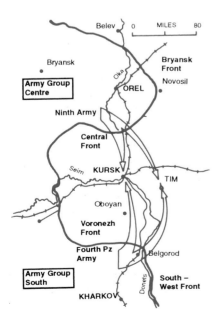

OPERATION *ZITADELLE* (CITADEL)

Although the front was now vastly extended and thinly held, Manstein's new positions offered to the German High Command the opportunity of an attack on the Soviet salient centred on Kursk. Code-named *Zitadelle*, the ensuing plan projected converging strikes on the northern and southern flanks of the salient to achieve a double envelopment. However, pre-warned of the German intentions by intelligence sources, General Zhukov was able to fortify the salient heavily. Both sides continued to build up their strength through the late spring and early summer and by the eve of the German attack some 2 million men and over 6,000 tanks were ready to go into action.

Grossdeutschland was formally redesignated as a Panzergrenadier division a week prior to the attack, on 23 June, and became almost identical in organisation to one of the elite SS Panzer divisions. During 1942 all the Army's infantry regiments had been renamed grenadier regiments and in 1943 the Infanterie-Divisions (mot) became Panzer-Grenadier-Divisions. However, the term Panzergrenadier is something of a misnomer, for in fact they were not always 'armoured', and would be better described as 'motorised infantry'.

Having been brought up to full strength for Zitadelle, the division began to the march to the staging area north of Tomarovka at the end of June 1943. The attack, launched on 4 July, saw the Ninth Army attack from the north and the Fourth Panzer Army from the south, across the base of the Soviet salient. GD attacked west of Strelazkoye with the 3rd and 11th Panzer Division, and initially made rapid advances. However, in the north the Ninth Army was stopped before a heavily fortified ridgeline on the 9th and the attack broke down, GD having advanced through the heavily defended Soviet lines as far as Kotschetovka.

On 12 July the Russians launched a strong counter-attack against the front north of Orel behind the Ninth Army. In the heavy fighting around Kalinovka, GD

PANZERGRENADIER DIVISION *GROSSDEUTSCHLAND*
as at September 1943

Div HQ
- (mot) Div Mapping Det
- Div Lorry Col
- Div Escort Coy
  - MC Platoon
  - Inf Gun Platoon
  - hy A/tk Platoon
  - SP Flak Platoon
  - Mixed PzJg Platoon

GD Grenadier and Fusilier Regiments
each of
Regt HQ and HQ Coy
- 1 x Sig Platoon
- 1 x Pioneer Platoon
- 1 x MC Platoon

1st Battalion
- Bn HQ
  - 3 x PzGr Coys
  - 1 x Hy Coy
    - 1 x HQ Pl
    - 1 x Mortar Pl
    - 1 x lt Inf Support Pl

2nd and 3rd (mot) Battalions
each of
Bn HQ
- 3 x PzGr Coys
- 1 x Hy Coy
  - 1 x Pioneer Pl
  - 1 x PzJg Pl
  - 1 x Inf Gun Sect
- 1 x MG Coy

4th SP Heavy Battalion
- Bn HQ
  - 1 x SP lt Flak Coy
  - 1 x SP Inf Gun Coy
  - 1 x SP Hy PzJg Coy

GD Panzer Regt
RHQ
- 1st Panzer Battalion
  - RHQ and HQ Coy
    - Flak Tank Pl
    - 4 x Panzer Pls (Panthers)

  - RHQ and HQ Coy
    - Flak Tank Pl
    - 4 x Panzer Pls (PzKpfwIVs)

  - RHQ and HQ Coy
    - 3 x Panzer Pls (Tigers)
    - 311th (FKL) Panzer Coy (assigned)

GD Panzer Recce Bn
Bn HQ
- 1 x SP Flak Pl
- 1 x AC Coy
- 1 x (halftrack) Recce Coy
- 2 x (wheeled) Recce Coys
- 1 x lt Panzer Recce Col
- 1 x hy Panzer Recce Coy
  - 1 x Pioneer Pl
  - 1 x med PzJg Pl
  - 1 x PzJg Pl
  - 1 x Inf Support Gun Sect

GD Panzerjäger Bn
Bn HQ
- 1 x SP Hy PzJg Coy
- 1 x (mot) Hy PzJg Coy

GD Sturmgeschütz Bn
Bn HQ, HQ Coy and HQ Bty
- 3 x Btys of 11 assault guns

GD Artillery Regiment
Regt HQ
- 1 x HQ Bty
- 1 x Observation Bty
- 1 x SP lt Flak Pl

1st Battalion
- HQ and HQ Bty
- 2 x (mot) 105mm Btys
- 1 x (mot) 150mm Bty

2nd Battalion
- HQ and SP HQ Bty
- 2 x SP lt Btys (each 6 x Wespe)
- 1 x SP hy Bty (6 x Hummel)

3rd Battalion
- HQ and (mot) HQ Bty
- 1 x (mot) 150mm Bty
- 1 x (mot) 105mm Bty
- 1 x (mot) 100mm Bty

4th Battalion
- HQ and (mot) HQ Bty
- 2 x (mot) 105mm Btys
- 1 x (mot) Bty (6 x Nebelwerfer)

GD Army Flak Battalion
Bn HQ and Bn Bty
- 3 x GD Hy Flak Coys
- 2 x GD SP med Flak Btys
- 1 x GD lt Flak Bty
- 1 x (mot) lt Flak Col

GD Feldersatz Bn
Bn HQ
- 5 x (mot) Coys

Signals Bn
Bn HQ
- 1 x Panzer Radio Coy
- 1 x (mot) Telephone Coy
- 1 x (mot) Lt Sigs Col

GD (mot) Pioneer Bn
Bn HQ
- 3 x (mot) Pioneer Coys
- 1 x (mot) Bridging Col
- 1 x (mot) lt Pioneer Col
- 1 x armd Pioneer Coy
- 1 x Pioneer Recce Pl

Supply Troops
HQ
- 1st–5th GD Transport Coys (120ton)
- 6th–8th GD Transport Coys (100ton)
- GD (mot) Supply Coy
- 3 x (mot) Maint Coys
- 1st–4th (mot) GD Maint Coys
- 1 x Maint Supply Sect

Admin Services
- 1 x Div Admin Office
- 1 x (mot) Butcher Coy
- 1 x (mot) Bakery Coy
- 1 x (mot) Fd Post Office
- 1 x MP Coy

Medical
- 3 x Ambulance Cols
- 2 x (mot) Med Coys
- 2 x (mot) Med Coys

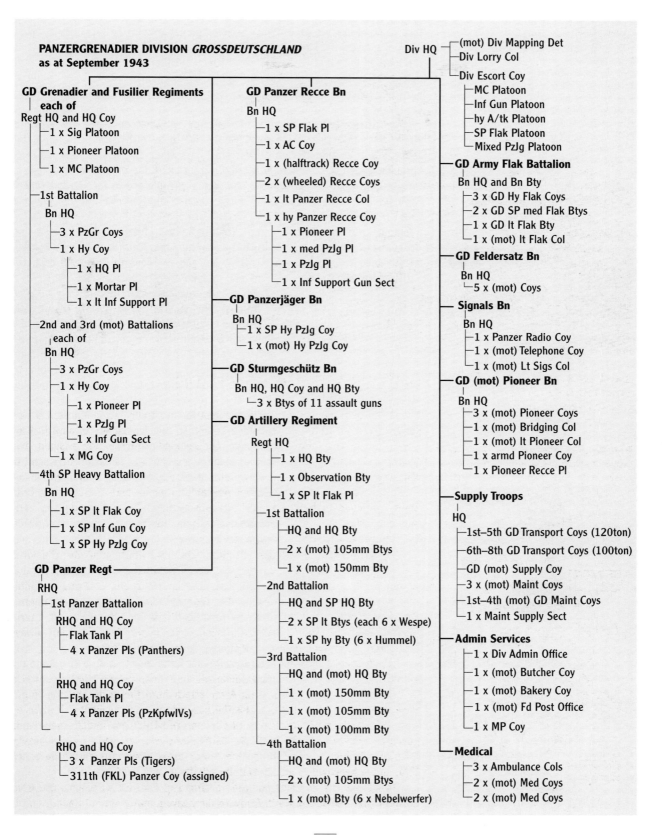

took heavy casualties, countering a series of Soviet armoured attacks in the second week of July. On the 17th, the division was relieved and transferred to Tamnoye to the south of the Kursk battlefield, by which point Hitler had been forced to concede defeat. Four days later GD moved again, by truck and rail, to the vicinity of Karachev, where it had fought the previous year, and was assigned to Army Group Centre.

Here it resisted the Russian advance from Bolkhov, until in early August a strong Russian attack in the south caused GD to be rushed south to join Army Group South at Akhtyrka on the Vorskla River, where the newly organised Tiger battalion joined the division. A fighting retreat along the central front continued through mid-August. The Russians had torn a 35-mile gap in the German line at Byelgorod, and through this they poured, heading south-west toward the Dnieper River. In their path, in positions to the east of Akhtyrka at Yankovka, Staraya Ryabina, Novaya Rabina and Yablotschnoye, Panzer-Grenadier-Division *Grossdeutschland* was slowly pushed back and by the 11th the men were fighting on the outskirts of Akhtyrka. At Akhtyrka, and positions to the south-east, GD battled hard, and for days with no rest, to counter the breakthrough.

Below: Operation *Zitadelle* was a disaster for the German forces in Russia. After expending men and tanks on the Russian defences, all their gains were swallowed up quickly as the Russians counter-attacked.

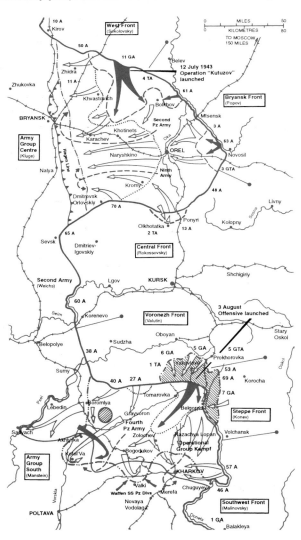

Kharkov fell on 23 August, and in the last week of August the Army Group Centre front was penetrated in three places by Malinovsky's forces and Tolbukhin's Southern Front, threatening an envelopment of Army Group South. Against Hitler's orders Manstein ordered Army Group South to withdraw to the Dnieper, and in so doing probably saved it.

Reassigned to the XLVIII Panzer Corps, GD was tasked in the first two weeks of September with reinforcing the weak points in the German line to the west of Kharkov and north of Poltava. As part of the general withdrawal, the division then began a skillful fighting retreat to Kremenchug, and the vital rail bridge there over the Dnieper. Fighting behind a progressively shorter line, the division had withdrawn into a pocket around the bridge by the 29th, and then began a general withdrawal over the river (among the last German troops to do so).

GD was now in a tenuous defensive position behind the Dnieper River, the strongest natural defensive line in western European Russia (but over which the Russian had five bridgeheads). In two and a half months Army Group Centre and South had been forced back for an average of 150 miles on a front 650 miles long. In so doing, the Germans had lost the most valuable territory they had taken in the Soviet Union.

In the first week of October, the Eastern Front was relatively quiet as the Russians regrouped and brought up new forces. Their numerical superiority allowed them to rest and refit their units in shifts, and they reached the Dnieper with their offensive capability largely intact.

Above: The original caption to this photograph boasts: 'The new German "Tiger" *Panzerkampfwagen*, the terror of our enemies! This tank is an outstanding achievement of the German armament technology. These steel giants clear the way on all fronts for our incomparable infantry.' Tigers were introduced to the Eastern Front around Leningrad in August 1942 and had an immediate impact on the battlefield.

Grossdeutschland, by contrast, had little time for rest. Reforming as separate detachments, the division was engaged in defensive battles for the first two weeks of October around the Russian-held Michurin-Rog bridgehead south of Kremenchung in support of the First and Eighth Panzer Armies. The Russians threw the full weight of the Second and Third Ukrainian Fronts against these two armies on 15 October, and opened a 200-mile-wide bridgehead between Cherkassy and Zaporozhe, while to the south the Third Ukrainian Front threatened important iron and manganese mining areas near Krivoi Rog and Nikopol. Hitler was determined to hold these at all costs.

In the first week of November, Kiev was retaken by the First Ukrainian Front, and the Fourth Panzer Army was pushed back west and south of the city, threatening to destroy the entire left flank of Army Group South, along which *Grossdeutschland* was ranged. Beginning in the middle of October, the division carried out a long and difficult retreat south and by the end of November was established on a line that stretched from Sofiyevka to Alexandrovka, to the east of Krivoi Rog.

December brought some respite, and the German forces were able to regain some of their balance. The best solution to the German predicament at this stage would have been to order Army Group South to withdraw to the next major line of defence, the Bug River, but this Hitler would not consider. Instead the armies were told to hold their positions for the winter, and informed that they would have to do so without extra resources since these were needed for defence against the expected invasion of north-west Europe.

In the third winter of the Russian campaign, the men of *Grossdeutschland* could reflect on a year in which they had received little or no rest, and had time and again been used to reinforce weak points in the German lines. Higher than average losses, many of them from the experienced core of veterans, were made good with new recruits, and despite the serious deterioration on all fronts during 1943, the division was able to keep its cohesion at a time when serious manpower shortages were forcing the Germans to field half strength divisions.

1944: THE BEGINNING OF THE END

On Christmas Eve 1943, on the southern flank of the German line, the First Ukrainian Front drove into the southern rim of the Fourth Panzer Army's positions around Kiev, and the next day it developed a second thrust west. Both threatened the envelopment of Army Groups South and A, but Manstein considered the southern thrust the greater danger, and ordered the Fourth Panzer Army to stop the Soviet armies from advancing south.

Grossdeutschland was soon in the thick of the action. Relieved at Krivoi Rog on 3 January, the unit was transferred to Kirovgrad in the path of the Soviet forces. Beginning from here it fought a continuing series of retreating defensive engagements until March. The First Ukrainian Front was approaching Uman by mid-January, but Hitler's insistence on holding the mines near Nikopol and Krivoi Rog meant that by the end of the month the Sixth Army had nearly been encircled. Also in mid-January, the 1st Battalion, 26th Panzer Regiment, equipped with Panther tanks, joined Panzer-Regiment *Grossdeutschland*. Later in the month, Generalleutnant Hoernlein, known affectionately by his troops as 'Papa', ceded command to the experienced Generalleutnant Manteuffel.

Between 27 January and 8 February a large part of the newly-reinforced Panzer-Regiment *Grossdeutschland* was transferred to the Cherkassy area, where Zhukov's First and Second Ukrainian Fronts had encircled two German corps. Together with most of Army Group South's tank strength, the unit succeeded in breaking half the trapped corps out on 17 February. Another element of the division, Kampfgruppe *Bohrend*, went to the Narva front on 5 February.

During early February the right flank of Army Group South was driven behind the 1939 Polish border nearly to Kovel. At the end of the month Army Groups South and A held a weak but almost continuous line about halfway between the Dnieper and the Bug.

In mid-February, with Army Group North retiring behind a fortified line (the Panther Line) and Army Groups South and A in comparatively stable positions, optimists in the German High

Below: Russian advances in the latter part of 1943 saw the Germans lose ground extensively in the Ukraine. 1944 would be a long, hard struggle for the men of Grossdeutschland.

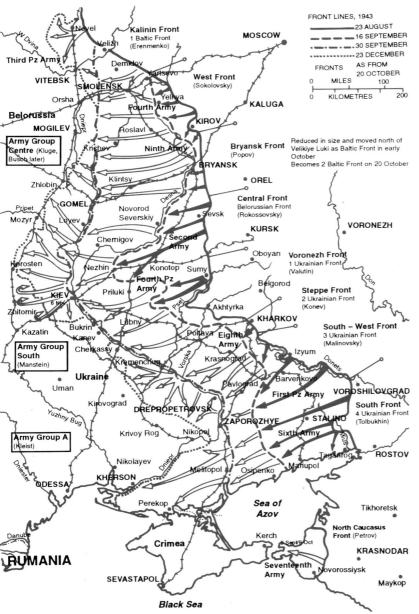

Command assumed that they had seen another winter through, and that, as in previous years, with the onset of spring, the front would sink into the mud for a month or so. The winter of 1943–44 was unusually warm and wet and therefore muddy, but even this did not prevent the Russians (whose own armour and transport, and that gifted by their Allies, were better able to move in mud) from advancing on all fronts.

During February the Soviet High Command shifted five of its six tank armies to the area opposite Army Group South, and by the end of the month another had appeared. On 4 March the First, Second and Third Ukrainian Fronts attacked the northern, central and southern flanks of Army Group South. *Grossdeutschland*, in positions west of Kirovgrad, met the onslaught of the Second Ukrainian Front, aimed at the centre of the Eighth Army east of Uman. Again the division was used to reinforce weak areas of the line, but by 15th had retreated south-west to Rovnoye.

The lack of manpower with which to meet the advance was a telling factor. So it was on all fronts. In Germany, measures were being taken to resolve the manpower crisis, but they were desperate and shortsighted. At the beginning of March, from the reinforcement forces of GD at Cottbus and Guben a Replacement Grenadier Regiment (mot) 1029 GD was raised. On 9 March, as the division withdrew under fire to the bend in the Bug River, Regiment 1029 GD transferred to Zakopane, and ten days later participated in the occupation of Hungary.

On 16 March the main body of the division began withdrawing all the way back to the Dniester River, via Pervomaisk, Ananjew, Voljadinka, and Rybniza. By the end of the month it had retreated into Romania, at Chisinau and Regiment 1029 GD was occupying Carpathian Mountain passes on the Hungarian–Romanian border at Kimpolung. The Soviets were now across the Prut River, having gained 165 miles on the three main thrust lines, and the German front was backed up against the Carpathians.

During early April, the Fourth Ukrainian Front launched an attack on the Crimea, trapping the German Seventeenth Army and forcing it into a small beachhead around Sevastopol. Despite these reversals, Germany was still far from beaten; Hitler had succeeded in his determination not to weaken the western defences for the sake of the east, German industrial output was still rising and tank and weapon production were sufficient to equip new divisions for the west and replace some of the losses in the east.

On the Carpathian front, *Grossdeutschland* fought defensive battles both east and west of Jassy in early April, during a gradual retreat to Targul Frumos in Bessarabia. The bitter fighting for the town continued for over a month, after which the front settled down to a period of relative quiet. During the respite, the Ist Battalion, Panzer-Füsilier-Regiment *Grossdeutschland* returned to Germany to equip with SPWs, and the armoured reconnaissance unit was also re-equipped. At

Above: Unloading essential equipment from an *'Tante Ju'* (Aunty Ju), a Junkers Ju52/3m transport aircraft, on an airfield somewhere on the Eastern Front.

Below: Tank recovery platoon in action. Two Hanomags attempt to pull a disabled SP gun from where it has become stuck in the mud, 26 June 1944.

Above: June 1944, a happy snap in front of a burning IS-2 Stalin tank of the man who knocked it out. Introduced in spring 1944, nearly 4,000 of these 122mm-armed monsters saw war service.

the same time, however, fusilier regiments were reduced to three battalions instead of four and each battalion was reduced from five companies to four.

At the beginning of June 1944, the Führer Escort Battalion was reinforced to regimental strength in East Prussia, and the main body of *Grossdeutschland* transferred to an area north of Podul on the Dniester. Here the division, reinforced on the 6th by returning elements of the Füsilier-Regiment, launched a counter-attack against Soviet forces. As it did so, the Allies launched Operation Overlord, the invasion of Northwest Europe. 1st Battalion, Panzer Regiment *Grossdeutschland*, in France converting to Panther tanks, was quickly thrown into the fighting around the Normandy beachhead.

After the fighting around Podul, the division moved to a rest area some 60 miles south of Jassy. The Füsilier-Regiment, freshly equipped with SPWs rejoined the division, and the Armoured Assault Engineer Battalion was reformed as an Armoured Assault Regiment. The short-lived Regiment 1029 was broken up and its men used to fill gaps in the ranks of other units of the division. After more than a month in the rear, the division was transferred in late July from Romania to East Prussia, to the area around Gumbinnen.

During the rest period, an attempt was made on Hitler's life by senior army officers. Seizing control of Berlin and its government quarter remained the pivotal goal of the conspirators and the immediate focal point of Operation Valkyrie. To accomplish the coup in Berlin, the army conspirators planned to use the troops of the *Grossdeutschland* Guard Battalion in Berlin, commanded by Otto Remer, and the personnel of the Infantry School in Döberitz, the Artillery School in Krampnitz, and Potsdam's 23rd Infantry. All SS and Gestapo offices in central Berlin, and Königswusterhausen radio station were top priority targets that were to be seized in the first hours of the intended coup. However, Remer stayed loyal to Hitler and, when it became known that the Führer had survived the bomb blast, the coup collapsed.

Above: Gunners from an artillery unit move behind their well-camouflaged howitzer to take up new positions, February 1944. Note rifle rack on rear of the 10.5mm le FH 18/40 light field howitzer.

Left: Winter in the East. Wrapped in blankets and wearing winter clothing, a mortar crew huddles in a shell crater, a shallow depression in the snow-covered terrain, trying to keep warm during a break in the fighting.

Opposite page: A typical *'Frontschweine'*, fatigued by the rigours of combat. He's wearing a standard issue field grey overcoat and leather belt and harness and carries a Karabiner 98k over his right shoulder.

Hitler and his staff fully expected that the Russians would renew their pressure on the southern flank and attempt to smash Army Group North Ukraine against the Carpathians. To meet this expected advance he transferred 80 per cent of Army Group Centre's armour to the south. Instead, the Russians struck north, at Army Group Centre, which held the last major stretch of Soviet territory left in German hands between Vitebsk and Orsha. Between 22 and 25 June they made deep penetrations across the whole front, and in less than two weeks 25 of the 38 Army Group Centre divisions were lost.

In July, the Soviet offensive spread to the flanks. In the north the First Baltic Front drove into the gap between Army Groups Centre and North toward East Prussia and the Baltic. On 29 July one of the Soviet spearheads reached the Baltic west of Riga and cut off Army Group North. On the southern flank of Army Group Centre, a two-pronged thrust aimed toward Brest-Litovsk carried the Soviets to Lublin and Warsaw. Only in August did the Soviet offensive subside, having outrun its supply lines.

In early August GD began an attack east from Gumbinnen toward the vicinity of

Right: Original German press release caption: 'The Messenger. The telephone wires have been destroyed, the radio is being used by the artillery—now is the time for a runner to get an important message to the next sector. The call "Messenger!" goes out. In the next moment he is standing in front of his company commander to receive the vital order. He knows what is at stake. In a scene reminiscent of the Great War, the Runner from the artillery unit splashes through deep muddy water at the bottom of a trench.'

Below: Russian advances in summer 1944.

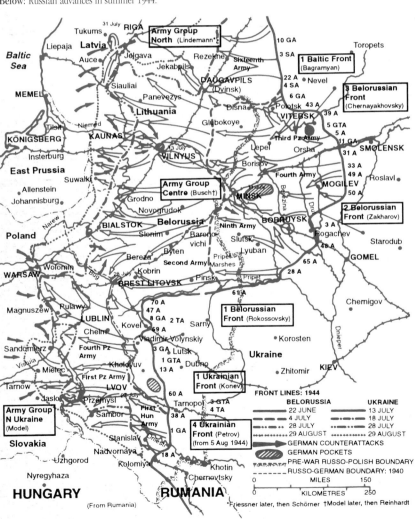

Wilkowischken (Wolfsburg) and Virballen, to take the initiative while the Soviet forces rested. The attack was a success, and Wilkowischen was taken. Soon, a new crisis arose in Lithuania, and the division marched to the area west of Schaulen (Siauliai) via Tauroggen, Kraziai, Kolainiai, and Luoke, for an attack to the east to prevent Soviet forces breaking through to the Baltic and cutting off the Kurland Front. On the 18th desperate battles to keep open this narrow land corridor to Army Group North began. Four days later, *Grossdeutschland* marched north and prepared for an attack towards Tukums, but this was halted on 25 August on the Lithuanian–Latvian border outside Doblen. After consolidating, the division then constructed defensive positions around Doblen, where it remained for the duration of September and into October.

At the beginning of September, Generalleutnant Manteuffel was replaced by Oberst Lorenz, commander of the Panzer-Grenadier-Regiment GD, and a month later the Guard Battalion in Berlin was expanded to regimental size.

Already, Army Group North had been forced to retreat to avoid being cut to pieces by an assault by the three Baltic fronts, and at the end of September had barely succeeded in escaping through the corridor south of

Riga that GD had fought to keep open. On 3 October parts of the division began transferring to the area west of Schaulen to meet the westward drive by the First Baltic Front. In the hard fought battles around Schaulen and Memel (Klaipeda) on the Baltic coast GD fought hard, but could do nothing to prevent the Russians from breaking through to the Baltic south of Memel on the 10th, cutting Army Group North off again in the Kurland. Around Memel, GD threw up a strong defensive perimeter that it was ordered to hold for more than a month, while the rest of the army group was evacuated from the port. Panzer-Regiment *Grossdeutschland*, attached to the 6th Panzer Division, was in action during the second week of October in the Rozan area of Poland.

During the summer and autumn the German position on all fronts had become increasingly desperate. On the Eastern Front, the focus of the Soviet summer offensive had swung back to the Balkans in mid-August, succeeded in retaking the vital Ploesti oilfields at the end of the month, and ended when Romania and Bulgaria capitulated. Finally, in October Belgrade was retaken. At the same time Allied troops were pushing the Germans steadily back through north-west Europe and Italy. Launching his last major offensive of the war against the Ardennes sector on the Western Front in December, Hitler failed in his plan to split the Allied armies and in the west began the retreat to the Fatherland. (For an account of the Führer Escort Brigade's participation in the Ardennes Offensive see below.)

Right: Grossdeutschland Tigers on the road to Iasi, Romania, May 1944.

Below: The Russian advance continues into central Europe.

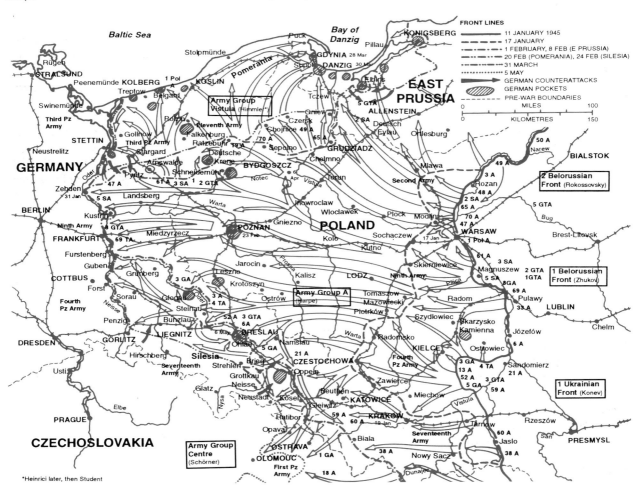

PANZER CORPS GROSSDEUTSCHLAND as at December 1944

Corps Staff
500th (mot) Mapping Det
500th (mot) MP Det
500th Recce Coy
500th (mot) Sound Ranging Pl
500th Escort Coy
500th Arty Bde Staff
500th (mot) Pioneer Regt Staff

Corps Troops
Fusilier Regt GD (2 x Bns and 1 x Inf Gun Coy)
Heavy Panzer Bn GD (HQ and HQ Coy,

1 x SP Flak PL, 3 x Tiger Coys, 1 x Maint Coy, 1 x Supply Coy)
500th Arty Regt (2 x Bns each of HQ and HQ Bty, 3 x (mot) Hy Btys)
500th Pz Pioneer Bn (HQ and HQ Coy, 3 x (mot) Pioneer Coys, 2 x (mot) Pz Bridging Cols)
44th Pz Sigs Bn (1 x Pz radio Coy, 1 x (mot) Sigs Coy, 2 x (mot) Telephone Coys, 1 x (mot) Sigs Supply Coy)
Pz Feldersatz Regt GD (2 x Bns each with 4 x Coys)

Pz Corps Support Troops (Supply Bn, Ordnance Bn, Motor Vehicle Maint Bn, Admin Troops Bn, 500th Med Bn, 500th (mot) Field Post office)

Fighting Troops
GD Panzergrenadier Division (inc PzRegt 1 of 3 Coys of 17 Panthers, PzRegt 2 of 4 Coys of 17 PzKpfwIVs) and Hy Pz Bn with Tigers.
BR Panzergrenadier Division
18th Arty Division

PANZER KORPS GROSSDEUTSCHLAND

In early November 1944 the OKH began reorganising Panzer-Grenadier-Division GD as Panzer-Korps GD by combining the division with the Panzer-Grenadier-Division *Brandenburg* (BR) and other units. It should be noted, however, that the Panzer-Korps GD never fought as a single unit, and its material strength was never comparable to that of a pre-1943 army corps.

In mid-November, the division was still holding its defensive positions around the Memel bridgehead. 1st Battalion, Panzer Regiment GD rejoined the division and 1st Battalion, Panzer Regiment 26, which had fought with GD while the former was in France, transferred to Hungary to fight attacks by the Second and Third Ukrainian Fronts against Budapest. On the 26th, the final evacuation of Memel began and GD was moved via boat through Königsberg (Kaliningrad) into the area around Rastenburg-Sensburg, to join the newly organised Panzer-Korps GD.

By the end of 1944, Germany's defeat had become inevitable. Throughout the year German forces had been almost continually on the defensive and now were fighting on home soil. GD had paid heavily in these defensive battles, and shortages in men and equipment were no longer made good. As an armoured corps, the main unit was continually pushed into the worst fighting, resulting in heavy casualties. Furthermore, the Training and Replacement Brigade had been vastly overburdened by the losses, and by the creation of the Führer-Begleit-Brigade and the Führer-Grenadier-Brigade, and as a result had virtually collapsed. To allay this crisis, the Training and Replacement Regiments of the Panzer-Grenadier-Division *Brandenburg* were attached to GD.

At the end of December of the fourth winter on the Eastern Front, *Grossdeutschland* was in camp near Hitler's headquarters at Rastenburg, resting and re-equipping for the defence of the Fatherland.

1945: THE FINAL ACT

In the first week of the new year, the division and the corps staff GD moved to the Willenberg area, where it was assigned as OKH reserve. On the 12th, Panzer-Grenadier-Division *Brandenburg* (commanded by Generalmajor Schulte-Heuthaus) was ordered to transfer to Lodz and along with the Luftwaffe Parachute Panzer Division *Hermann Göring* was placed under the command of the corps staff *Grossdeutschland*, and its commander General der Panzertruppe Saucken.

The final Soviet offensive of the war was launched on 12 January, with the bulk of the effort concentrated against the northern front, towards East Prussia, Silesia and Pomerania. Soviet leaders hoped that early and deep penetrations could then be exploited by a drive across Poland to the Oder River. From the 15th to the 30th, GD fought a series of defensive actions in northern Poland, but could not contain the advance of the Second and Third White Russian Fronts, driving west from

Below: Fatigue apparent on their faces, these troops are rotated after a period of sustained fighting.

Ebenrode and north-west of Warsaw, and was forced to retreat north into an area south of Königsberg in East Prussia.

During the same period, the *Brandenburg* Division was transferred to the Lodz–Piotrkov area in Poland to meet the First White Russian Front advancing south of Warsaw, but to avoid being encircled by the two arms of the attack, began retreating west out of its positions to the Neisse River north of Görlitz.

Then began a complex and ultimately fruitless period of reorganisation, as successive Panzer-Korps *Grossdeutschland* units were expanded. On 20 January the Army Tank Destroyer Force GD was formed by Panzergrenadier Replacement Brigade GD in Cottbus, and went into action on the Oder River at Steinau. The Führer-Grenadier-Brigade was transferred to a rest centre south of Arzfeld after months of heavy fighting. On 26 January Panzer-Grenadier-Division *Kurmark* (KMK) was formed from various Kampfgruppen and extemporised units of the GD Replacement Brigade (for a full account of this unit's history see below), and on the 30th the OKH ordered the Führer-Begleit-Brigade and Führer-Grenadier-Brigade expanded to full Panzer divisions, these becoming Führer-Begleit-Division (FBD) and Führer-Grenadier-Division (FGD) respectively.

At the end of January *Grossdeutschland* was engaged in heavy fighting in East Prussia, where it had retreated in the face of the Russian steamroller to positions around Bischofsburg and Braunswalde. In early May, the Guard Regiment *Grossdeutschland* became the Field Guard Regiment *Grossdeutschland* and went into action near Kustrin, while the FGD (newly refitted at Koblenz) and FBD were transferred to Stargard and Freienwalde respectively for an attack on Stargard. This was launched on 12 February, but lacking the strength that the units' spurious divisional status suggested, it was only successful in stabilising the front and captured little territory.

Above: Troops reload a camouflaged six-barrelled Nebelwerfer rocket-launcher. Originally designed to lay smoke (thus the name), the 15cm Nebelwerfer 41 on a two-wheeled carriage was the main version.

Above: During a pause in the fighting, the crew of a light 37mm anti-aircraft gun prepare a meal.

Above right: The Russians surround Berlin.

Below right: Two Tigers prior to a local counter-attack. This photograph gives an excellent close-up of the turret front and front of the tank. Note the machine gun, driver's armoured viewing slit and smoke dischargers on either side of the turret.

On the 12th, in recognition of the growing crisis on the Eastern Front, the 'Emergency' Brigade GD was organised at Cottbus from the GD Replacement Brigade. (It subsequently went into action at Forst on the Oder River, and was taken over by the *Brandenburg* Division on 10 March.)

The Oder was the last natural line of defence before Berlin, but by 3 February, the First White Russian Front was on the river only 35 miles east of Germany's capital. To the south, the First Ukrainian Front began attacking across the Oder north of Breslau (Wroclaw) on 8 February. What was left of the GD replacement units stationed at Guben near Görlitz were then thrown into the battles between Forst and the Czech border area, as the Panzer-Korps *Grossdeutschland* fought to contain the advance of the First Ukrainian Front to the Neisse River.

Through January and February, the *Grossdeutschland* Grenadier and Fusilier Regiments were slowly pushed back into a defensive pocket on the Fritsches Haff (Bay). By the end of March only 4,000 men remained, and on the 29th the survivors were evacuated from the port of Balga to Pillau by ferry, almost immediately going into combat in the Samland. Further south, in the last week of February, through March and into the second week of April, desperate defensive battles were fought by the *Brandenburg* Division on the Neisse River between Muskau and Steinbach.

In late March, the GD replacement units not engaged in combat were transferred to Schleswig-Holstein and Denmark. In early March, the action on the Neisse slackened, and the focus of action transferred to the south in front of Hungary. On 10 March both FGD and FBD were again relieved and transferred, to Angermünde and Langenoeis respectively. On 15 March FGD went back into combat near Stettin (Szczecin) on the Oder.

In a final flurry of reorganisation, the Panzergrenadier Combat Force *Grossdeutschland* was formed from the GD replacement forces in Denmark and Schleswig-Holstein on 23 March. PGD *Kurmark*, which had been fighting on the Oder north of Frankfurt since the end of February, was relieved and sent to rest behind the front lines on 28 March.

The Russians regrouped on the Oder-Neisse line in April, the Second White Russian Front in the north, the First White Russian in the centre opposite Berlin and the First Ukrainian Front (under Konev) in the south. This last force faced the core of GD and BR across the Neisse on the night of 15 April. The attack fell on the 16th, and in the south the division could not prevent a breakthrough by the vastly numerically superior Soviet armies on the first day.

In early April, both the FGD and FBD were transferred to Vienna, Austria. The newly created Panzergrenadier Combat Force GD entered combat at Lingen on the Ems River and was later absorbed by the 15th Panzergrenadier Division.

Although it was clear to all by mid-April that the war had now become little more than a pointless personal crusade by the Führer, the divisions continued to fight on. In the last two weeks of the month *Kurmark* engaged in very heavy defensive fighting between the Oder and Halbe, and the few remnants of GD were largely destroyed or dispersed in heavy retreating battles at Pillau. The last survivors of GD were able to cross the Hela peninsula and from there go via Bornholm to Schleswig-Holstein. FBD was destroyed in battles east of, and in the area of Spremberg, although some survivors were able to make it back to Panzer-Korps GD

BR and Panzer-Korps GD were engaged in heavy, costly defensive fighting and retreat between the Neisse River and Dresden. On 1 May BR was transferred to the Olmutz area, from where it fought to escape encirclement between the 3rd and 9th

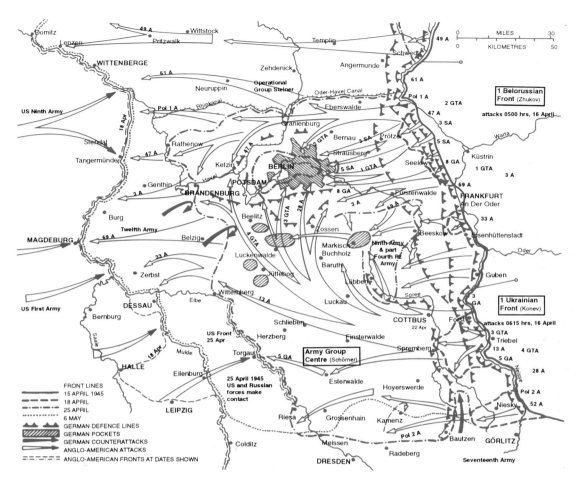

FRONT LINES
15 APRIL 1945
18 APRIL
25 APRIL
6 MAY
GERMAN DEFENCE LINES
GERMAN POCKETS
GERMAN COUNTERATTACKS
ANGLO-AMERICAN ATTACKS
ANGLO-AMERICAN FRONTS AT DATES SHOWN

Above: An Army flak-artillery unit—twin 37mm guns on a halftrack. An Army Flak Battalion was provided for most motorised infantry divisions from September 1943.

Right: Laying Teller mines on a muddy road in the Pripet swamp area.

Opposite page, above: Heavy self-propelled artillery fording a river somewhere on the Eastern Front, 11 May 1944.

Opposite page, below: Tigers grouping on a reverse slope for a counter-attack. *Grossdeutschland* received the Tiger before many other units, having a Tiger battalion from summer 1943.

Above: Troops snatch a mid-day meal break crouching in their trench mortar position.

Right: German grenadiers dismount from a Sturmgeschütz.

to Deutschbrod. In the battle for Berlin between 19 April and 5 May the Guard Regiment GD was all but wiped out. On the 7th Germany signed an unconditional surrender at Reims, repeating the process on the 9th in Berlin. Some 2,000,000 German soldiers passed into Soviet captivity, including most of Panzer-Korps *Grossdeutschland* and all of FGD (which was turned over under agreement after surrendering to the Americans). Those that survived Soviet captivity only returned years later.

THE PANZER DIVISION 'KURMARK'

In January 1945 following the massive Soviet offensive on the Vistula, *Grossdeutschland* Panzer Corps, along with other units from Hungary and the Western Front were ordered to bolster up the section of front in the vicinity of Fourth Panzer Army. The Soviet Army was now advancing on the Oder and such was the speed of the advance that, having raced across the Vistula, it had broken the German front line in several places. XI and XXIV Panzer Corps were sent to restore some semblance of order to the German front but the Soviets launched a strong counter-attack on the German forces and surrounded XXIV Panzer Corps. cutting it off in a pocket.

Grossdeutschland was sent to rescue the trapped units, but the front around them was crumbling. In response, the OKH was prompted to created some large Kampfgruppen to provide greater flexibility in defence. One of these new battle groups, Kampfgruppe *Langkeit* under the command of Oberst Willi Langkeit, was formed on 3 February 1945 and was made up from the Corps Panzergrenadier Replacement Brigade which was almost at full strength and Alarm Group *Schmeltzer*. It was organised as a Type 44 Panzergrenadier Division, with its Panzergrenadier battalions organised on the 1945 model, with three self-propelled gun companies equipped with Jagdpanzer 38s and one company with Pz Mk IVs. The artillery battalion was organised from the 3rd Battalion, 184th (mot) Artillery Regiment. The Panzergrenadier regiment apparently had only a staff, a staff company, and two Panzergrenadier battalions. The order of 4 February 1945 gave the division an authorised strength of 4,559 men including 128 Hiwis.

They were sent into action on 27 January at Sternberg to free the trapped German units, which included SS-Oberführer Wilhelm Bittrich's SS Panzer Corps. On 30 January Langkeit sent in the 2nd Battalion of his Kampfgruppe which, after some heavy fighting around Pinnow, made contact with the SS troops, joining up with them as they retreated towards Frankfurt. Langkeit's troops were to defend Reppen which was the position the Soviets were advancing on to outflank the main body of his battle group.

When it became evident to Langkeit that the Soviets were about to outflank him and there was no realistic chance of advancing to Sternberg he decided to move towards Reppen in order to reinforce the 2nd Battalion. This journey was hampered by refugees who clogged the roads with carts and other forms of transport and when a Soviet attack met the battle group head on many civilians died in the resulting battle. It was evident that they were almost surrounded and Langkeit ordered a breakout through the nearby woods. Again they met Soviet resistance and even an attack by a squadron of Hans Ulrich Rudel's tank-busting Stukas did not help matters much.

Eventually, on 3 February, the Soviet line was broken with the aid of tank destroyers of Langkeit's battle group and men and armour as well as some civilian refugee columns poured through the gap, all heading in the direction of Frankfurt.

PANZERGRENADIER DIVISION KURMARK AS AT 14 FEBRUARY 1945

Div HQ

- **Kurmark Panzer Battalion**
  HQ and HQ Coy
  - HQ Pl
  - Panzer Flak Pl
  - Panzer Platoon

  - 3 x Panzer Coys (14 StuGs)
  - 1 x Panzer Coy (10 PzKpfwIVs)
  - Panzer Maint Pl
  - (mot) Panzer Supply Coy

- **Luftwaffe Flak Bn**
  - Bn HQ and (mot) HQ Bty
    - 3 (mot) Hy Flak Coys
    - 1 (mot) Mixed Flak Bty

- **Kurmark Panzergrenadier Regiment**
  - RHQ and HQ Coy
    - Sigs Pl
    - MC Pl
    - PzJg Pl
  - 1st (mot) Battalion
    Bn HQ
    - 1 x (mot) PzGr Supply Coy
    - 3 x (mot) PzGr Coys
    - 2 x (mot) Heavy Coy

  - 2nd (mot) Battalion
    Bn HQ
    - 1 x (mot) PzGr Supply Coy
    - 3 x (mot) PzGr Coys
    - 2 x (mot) Heavy Coy

  - Maintenance Platoon

  - (mot) Mixed Signals Coy

- **Kurmark Recce Bn**
  - Recce Coy

- **Kurmark PzJr Bn**
  - PzJr Coy

- **Kurmark Arty Regt**
  - Ist Battalion
    - HQ and (mot) HQ Bty
    - 3 x (mot) Btys

  - 2nd Battalion
    assigned, not present

- **Kurmark Pioneer Bn**
  - Bn HQ
    - (mot) Pioneer Supply Coy
    - 2 x (mot) Pioneer Coys

FÜHRER BEGLEIT (ESCORT) BRIGADE as at the Battle of the Bulge

Expanded to a Brigade in November 1944, the Führer Begleit Brigade's order of battle was:

Bde HQ and HQ Coy
   (1 x halftrack Inf Pl, 1 x halftrack Flak Pl)

Brigade troops
   (1 x AC Recce Coy, 1 x Sigs Coy, 1 x Flak Coy, 1 x Pioneer Coy, 1 x SP Gun Coy, 1 x SP PzJg Coy)

Führer Begleit Panzergrenadier Regiment
   (HQ Coy, 1 x Pz Fusilier Bn, 1 x (mot) PzGr Bn)

829th Infantry Battalion
   (3 x Rifle Coys, 1 x Hy Coy, 1 x Supply Coy)

Führer Begleit Panzer Battalion
   (HQ 2 x Panther Coys, 1 x Jagdpanther Coy, 1 x PzJg Coy, 1 x StuG Coy, 1 x Supply Coy, 1 x Maint Coy)

Führer Begleit Sturmgeschütz Brigade
   (HQ and HQ Bty, 3 x StuG Btys of 10 StuGs each)

Führer Begleit Artillery Regiment
   (2 x Bns of Bn HQ and HQ Bty, 3 x halftrack Btys, 1 x Supply Bty; FB Flak Bn of 3 Btys)

Führer Begleit Battle School
   (HQ and 3 (mot) Coys)

2 x Ambulance Pls

1 x (mot) Med Coy

1 (mot) Maint Coy

2 x Transport Cols

The jaws of the pocket that had been breached were held open by the 2nd Battalion with additional artillery support from artillery units situated in nearby Damm, a suburb of Frankfurt. Part of Kampfgruppe *Langkeit* remained here while the rest was ordered to cross the River Oder. On 3 February Kampfgruppe *Langkeit* was re-formed with new armoured vehicles including new Panther tanks and was renamed the Panzer-Division *Kurmark*.

The division was deployed on the Oder River where the three advancing Soviet fronts had stalled after over-extending their supply lines and it was *Kurmark*'s task to deny the Soviets the high ground east of the Oder which they would need to reconnoitre the whole of the Frankfurt sector. This they did and as a result Soviet attacks in this sector were beaten back. It was not until 16 April that the last Soviet

Right: A Füsilier takes up position ready to fire his *Panzerfaust*—'Armoured Fist'. This close-combat anti-tank weapon was produced in a number of versions with ranges from 30m to 150m and in massive quantities (around eight million of all types from mid-1943 onwards).

offensive was launched, and under the massive Soviet onslaught the units protecting *Kurmark*'s flanks crumbled, resulting in the division being surrounded. All attempts to rescue the trapped division failed.

Ninth Army fell back to the River Spree on 21 April with its units dispersed and unable to fight as a cohesive whole. *Kurmark* was one of these units, by now engaged in heavy combat in the Colpin woods. Halbe was chosen as the point at which a breakout was to be attempted but well positioned pockets of Soviet artillery and armour prevented the planned breakout. The fighting that took place at Halbe was vicious and intense with hand to hand combat as *Kurmark* desperately tried to break the Soviet ring. The division fought in vain as the Soviets had covered every escape route and at Halbe *Kurmark* ceased to exist as a fighting unit. Very few survivors made it out and those that did had to battle their way to the Elbe where there were American positions near Jerichow. Only 30,000 Germans from an entire army made it to the safety of American captivity.

THE FÜHRER BEGLEIT DIVISION

From 1938 a unit from the Wachregiment Berlin was assigned to guard Hitler and did so until the attempt on his life on 20 July 1944. The men for this bodyguard were drawn from the Wachregiment Berlin and then from the *Grossdeutschland* Regiment. They escorted Hitler throughout the Polish campaign and formed the cadre for the Führer-Begleit-Bataillon that was created in October 1939. This followed Hitler throughout the campaign in France. In the aftermath a detachment was sent to Hendaye on the Spanish border as a bodyguard for Hitler during his talks with Spain's General Franco, the remainder staying in Paris to act as official escort for dignitaries. A year later in June 1941, when Hitler moved his HQ to Rastenburg in East Prussia, the Escort Battalion was assigned to guard him there.

To gain some military experience (and credibility) the Kampfgruppe *Nehring* was formed, into which men from the Führer Escort Battalion were rotated for three-month periods of front line duty. The crisis that developed on the Eastern Front during the first Russian winter forced the Kampfgruppe to stay at the front, due to the fact it was about the only well equipped reserve available. As a result of this development the Kampfgruppe was increased in size with the addition of a Panzer company, anti-tank company, motor-cycle and flak platoon, as well as signals and other support units.

Despite this expansion Kampfgruppe *Nehring* never fought as a complete unit under the one command but was split into several small detachments. This resulted in serious losses and it was withdrawn from the front line at the end of March 1942.

In the winter offensive of 1942–43 the Soviets drove through Second Army's sector of the front and among the units sent to hold the line were a heavy weapons company, Panzer company and rifle company of the Führer Escort Battalion. They performed well, and later at Kharkov nearly the whole of Führer Escort Battalion was committed to action with the *Grossdeutschland* Division with a minimal guard being left at the Wolfschanze. The

Below: Sturmgeschütz 40 Ausf G assault guns, most with 'skirts' fitted as a defence against hollow-charged weapons, line-up on a dirt road somewhere on the Eastern Front awaiting orders to advance, December 1943.

Above: The 88mm Panzerschreck close-combat anti-tank weapon was a copy of the American M1 bazooka, first seen in Tunisia. With a range of 150m, it was operated by a two-man team and proved very effective from its introduction in 1943.

Right: Panthers from *Grossdeutschland*—now a Panzer division—are accompanied by a Panzergrenadier carrying an MG 34 during an action on 12 August 1944.

battalion was finally returned to the Wolfschanze in Rastenburg in April 1943 and from it the Führer-Grenadier Division was later raised.

In late 1943 the Soviets opened their third winter offensive. On the Narva Front Army Group North suffered heavy losses and Hitler ordered a Begleit Kampfgruppe to secure the main highway and guard the sea flank from a Soviet seaborne landing. This it did successfully.

On its return to Rastenburg it was suggested that the battalion be expanded to regimental size and kept on permanent standby as a type of 'fire brigade' to be rushed into critical spots at the front. The battalion was subsequently sent to Berchtesgaden and expanded to regimental size with additional manpower from Panzergrenadier Replacement Brigade *Grossdeutschland*. Following the 20 July Bomb Plot Oberst Remer was appointed field commander of the new regiment with Oberst Streve appointed the HQ commander.

On 27 November the Führer Escort Battalion was reinforced to armoured brigade status (Führer-Begleit-Brigade—FBB) and transferred from East Prussia into the Eifel, under Oberst Remer and sent west for the Ardennes Offensive. Stationed on the right flank of the Fifth Panzer Army, it was involved in heavy combat with US forces. On 30 January 1945 the regiment was officially upgraded to divisional status and in February was sent to the Oder Front in company with its sister division the Führer Grenadier Division. Both were involved in very heavy combat against the Soviet Army and the Führer Escort Division was eventually encircled at Spremburg. After a fierce breakout attempt on 21 April 1945 only a handful of survivors remained.

INFANTRY DIVISION/PANZER CORPS *GROSSDEUTSCHLAND*'S RUSSIAN WAR

Date	Corps	Army	Army Group	Area
6.42	Reserve	–	South	Kursk
7.42	XXXXVIII	2nd Army	South	Voronezh
8.42	–	1st Pz Army	A	Manytsch
9.42–11.42	–	9th Army	Centre	Rzhev
12.42	XXIII	9th Army	Centre	Rzhev
1.43	–	9th Army	Centre	Smolensk
2.43	Cramer	–	B	Charkow
3.43–4.43	–	Kempf	South	Charkow
5.43	refreshing	–	–	South Poltava, Karkov
6.43–7.43	XXXXVIII	4th Pz Army	South	Achtyrka, Obojan
8.43	XXIII	2nd Pz Army	Centre	Bryansk
9.43	XXXXVIII	4th Pz Army	South	Krementschug
10.43–12.43	LVII	1st Pz Army	South	Krivoi-Rog
1.44	XXX	6th Army	South	Kirovograd
2.44	LII	8th Army	South	Kirovograd
3.44	XXX	8th Army	South	Kirovograd
4.44–5.44	LVII	8th Army	South Ukraine	Jassy
6.44	refreshing	4th Rumanian Army	South Ukraine	Bacau/Sereth
7.44	reserve	–	South Ukraine	Bacau/Sereth
8.44–9.44	XXXXIX	3rd Pz Army	Centre	Lithuania
10.44–12.44	XXVIII	3rd Pz Army	Centre	Memel
1.45	reorganising	OKH	–	Rastenburg
2.45–3.45	Hermann Goring Corps	4. Army	North	Konigsberg, Pillau
4.45	IX	East Prussia	–	Samland

Above: These men relax in the shade of their shelter quarters (*Zeltbanen*) joined to form a tent supported from the canvas muzzle cover of their Sturmgeschütz.

Left: Flames erupt from a burning T-34 as a self-propelled gun roars past. Based on the PzKpfw 38(t) this is armed with a 75mm PAK 40/3.

Opposite page, above: Painted with in an unusual camouflage scheme, this Marder III passes Hungarian infantry moving forward somewhere in the Upper Dniester and Carpathian area of fighting, May 1944.

Opposite page, below: A hole in the ground, rifle, entrenching tool and field telephone—that is the world of this forward observation post of an artillery battery from *Grossdeutschland* somewhere on the Eastern Front.

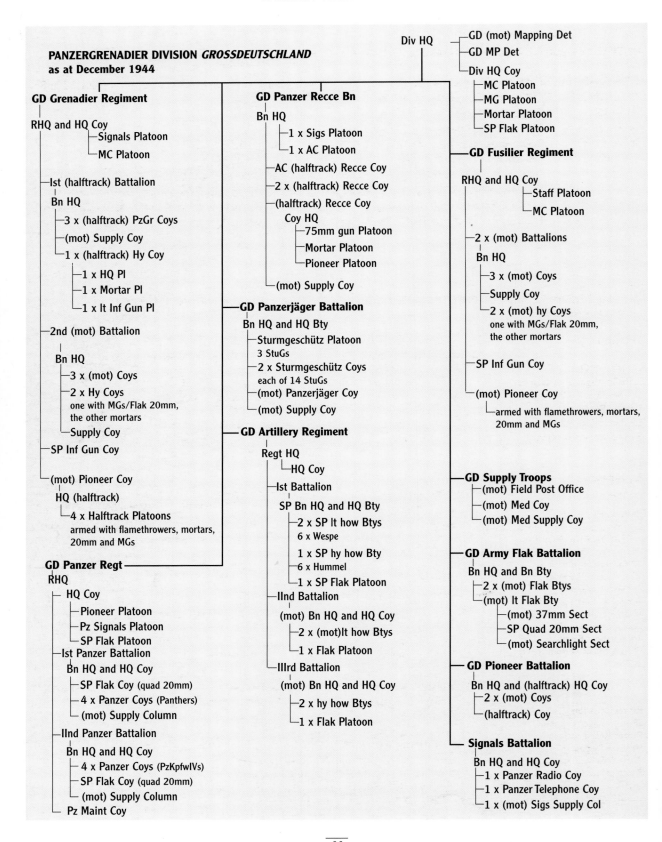

PANZERGRENADIER DIVISION *GROSSDEUTSCHLAND*
as at December 1944

Div HQ
- GD (mot) Mapping Det
- GD MP Det
- Div HQ Coy
  - MC Platoon
  - MG Platoon
  - Mortar Platoon
  - SP Flak Platoon

GD Grenadier Regiment

RHQ and HQ Coy
- Signals Platoon
- MC Platoon

- 1st (halftrack) Battalion
- Bn HQ
  - 3 x (halftrack) PzGr Coys
  - (mot) Supply Coy
  - 1 x (halftrack) Hy Coy
    - 1 x HQ Pl
    - 1 x Mortar Pl
    - 1 x lt Inf Gun Pl

- 2nd (mot) Battalion
- Bn HQ
  - 3 x (mot) Coys
  - 2 x Hy Coys
    one with MGs/Flak 20mm,
    the other mortars
  - Supply Coy
- SP Inf Gun Coy

- (mot) Pioneer Coy
  HQ (halftrack)
  - 4 x Halftrack Platoons
    armed with flamethrowers, mortars,
    20mm and MGs

GD Panzer Regt

RHQ
- HQ Coy
  - Pioneer Platoon
  - Pz Signals Platoon
  - SP Flak Platoon
- lst Panzer Battalion
  Bn HQ and HQ Coy
  - SP Flak Coy (quad 20mm)
  - 4 x Panzer Coys (Panthers)
  - (mot) Supply Column
- IInd Panzer Battalion
  Bn HQ and HQ Coy
  - 4 x Panzer Coys (PzKpfwIVs)
  - SP Flak Coy (quad 20mm)
  - (mot) Supply Column
- Pz Maint Coy

GD Panzer Recce Bn

Bn HQ
- 1 x Sigs Platoon
- 1 x AC Platoon
- AC (halftrack) Recce Coy
- 2 x (halftrack) Recce Coy
- (halftrack) Recce Coy
  Coy HQ
  - 75mm gun Platoon
  - Mortar Platoon
  - Pioneer Platoon

- (mot) Supply Coy

GD Panzerjäger Battalion

Bn HQ and HQ Bty
- Sturmgeschütz Platoon
  3 StuGs
- 2 x Sturmgeschütz Coys
  each of 14 StuGs
- (mot) Panzerjäger Coy
- (mot) Supply Coy

GD Artillery Regiment

Regt HQ
- HQ Coy
- lst Battalion
  SP Bn HQ and HQ Bty
  - 2 x SP lt how Btys
    6 x Wespe
  - 1 x SP hy how Bty
    6 x Hummel
  - 1 x SP Flak Platoon
- IInd Battalion
  (mot) Bn HQ and HQ Coy
  - 2 x (mot)lt how Btys
  - 1 x Flak Platoon
- IIIrd Battalion
  (mot) Bn HQ and HQ Coy
  - 2 x hy how Btys
  - 1 x Flak Platoon

GD Fusilier Regiment

RHQ and HQ Coy
- Staff Platoon
- MC Platoon

- 2 x (mot) Battalions
  Bn HQ
  - 3 x (mot) Coys
  - Supply Coy
  - 2 x (mot) hy Coys
    one with MGs/Flak 20mm,
    the other mortars

- SP Inf Gun Coy

- (mot) Pioneer Coy
  - armed with flamethrowers, mortars,
    20mm and MGs

GD Supply Troops
- (mot) Field Post Office
- (mot) Med Coy
- (mot) Med Supply Coy

GD Army Flak Battalion

Bn HQ and Bn Bty
- 2 x (mot) Flak Btys
- (mot) lt Flak Bty
  - (mot) 37mm Sect
  - SP Quad 20mm Sect
  - (mot) Searchlight Sect

GD Pioneer Battalion

Bn HQ and (halftrack) HQ Coy
- 2 x (mot) Coys
- (halftrack) Coy

Signals Battalion

Bn HQ and HQ Coy
- 1 x Panzer Radio Coy
- 1 x Panzer Telephone Coy
- 1 x (mot) Sigs Supply Col

HISTORY OF PANZER *GROSSDEUTSCHLAND* ERSATZ (REPLACEMENT) BRIGADE

1 June 1942	Formed as GD's training unit with constituent elements GD (mot) Infantry Ersatz Regt and GD Artillery Ersatz Bn.
10 Feb 1943	Fast Troop Training Battalion included (ceases end 1943).
Feb 1945	Sees action near Forst.
10 Mar 1945	Used to restore Brandenburg PzGdr Division.
Spring 1945	Reformed as PzGdr Ersatz und Ausbildungs Brigade GD.
4 Apr 1945	Reorganised on paper to include:

GD Panzer Ausbildungs Battalion, GD Panzergrenadier Ausbildungs Regiment (3 x Abteilungen), GD Officer Candidate School, GD Panzer Artillery Ausbildungs Battalion, GD Panzer Pioneer Ausbildungs Battalion (2 x Coys), GD Panzer Signals Ausbildungs Battalion (1 x Coy), 20th Panzer Ausbildungs Battalion. Taken into 15th PzGdr Division, it surrendered to the British at the end of the war.

OFFICIAL PERSONNEL AND EQUIPMENT ESTABLISHMENT OF A TYPE 1944 PANZERGRENADIER DIVISION
as at 1 August 1944

Personnel

	Officers	Other Ranks		Officers	Other Ranks
Division HQ	23	168	Artillery Regiment	48	1,522
2 PzGr Regiments total of	150	6,064	Army Flak Battalion	18	617
(inc 3 x PzGr Bn each of	20	848)	(mot) Pioneer Battalion	17	816
Panzer Battalion	21	581	(mot) Signals Battalion	13	414
SP Panzerjäger Battalion	17	458	Replacement Battalion	17	956
Panzer Recce Battalion	23	982	Others (Medical, Admin, etc)	23	1,039
			TOTAL	370	13,617

Equipment

	HMGs	LMGs	75mm Pak40	80mm mortar	120mm mortar	20mm flak	150mm hy gun	flame-thrower	20mm SP quad
Division HQ	0	4	0	0	0	0	0	0	0
2 Panzergrenadier Regiments total of	28	182	6	16	24	36	8	36	0
(inc 3 x PzGr Bn each of	12	66	0	6	12	18	0	0	0
Panzer Battalion	0	0	0	0	0	0	0	0	3
SP Panzerjäger Battalion	0	21	12	0	0	0	0	0	0
Panzer Recce Battalion	12	48	0	12	0	0	0	0	0
Artillery Regiment	0	44	0	0	0	0	0	0	0
Army Flak Battalion	0	10	0	6	0	10	0	0	0
(mot) Pioneer Battalion	0	57	0	6	0	0	0	0	0
(mot) Signals Battalion	0	13	0	0	0	0	0	0	0
Replacement Battalion	12	68	1	6	2	1	0	2	0
Others (Medical, Admin, etc)	0	14	0	0	0	0	0	0	0
TOTAL	52	461	19	46	26	47	8	38	3

	PzBef WglV	AC	StuG 75mm	PzJglV 75mm	20mm	105mm leFH	150mm sFH	100mm gun	88mm gun	37mm flak	20mm SP
Panzer Battalion	3	4	42	0	0	0	0	0	0	0	0
SP Panzerjäger Battalion	0	0	0	31	0	0	0	0	0	0	0
Panzer Recce Battalion	0	17 hy*	0	0	0	0	0	0	0	0	0
Artillery Regiment	0	0	0	0	9	36	12	6	0	0	0
Army Flak Battalion	0	0	0	0	6	0	0	0	8	9	3
Replacement Battalion	0	0	0	0	0	1	0	0	0	0	0
TOTAL	3	21	42	31	15	37	12	6	8	9	3

*or 20 light. Armament 16 LMGs, 13 20mm, 3 75mm guns.

INSIGNIA & MARKINGS

Opposite page:
Above: Typical army shoulders straps with the Gothic 'W' insignia for the 'Wach' in Wachtruppe or Wachregiment Berlin, and the entwined letters 'GD' for *Grossdeutschland*.

Below left: A soldier of the Wachregiment Berlin, showing off the Gothic 'W' insignia on his shoulders strap.

Below right: The commander of an armoured engineer battalion pins tank destruction badge—*Panzervernichtungsabzeichen*—to the arm of a Pionier Obergefreiter. In the background is the Soviet T-34 destroyed by this young soldier. Note the *Grossdeutschland* cuff title.

Below: The three main *Grossdeutschland* cuff titles.

Like all German units, *Grossdeutschland* used extensive vehicle markings and uniform insignia to distinguish it on the battlefield. There was, of course, great variety in the type of personal equipment with which the individual soldier might be issued, but like all armies a large degree of uniformity existed.

GROSSDEUTSCHLAND INSIGNIA

The German Army had a complex system of uniform colouring that was used to distinguish soldiers from different types of units. This colouring was used as piping and edging or *Waffenfarbe* (arm of service colours) on the uniform and, as the name suggests, was determined by the soldier's arm of service. Infantrymen wore white Waffenfarbe, and engineers wore black. Various devices were used along with the Waffenfarbe to distinguish the individual unit to which the soldier belonged. *Grossdeutschland* wore white Waffenfarbe with an entwined 'GD'.

The German Army also had specialist badges, which were worn by soldiers under the rank of Leutnant. The badges were either worn on the lower right, upper left, or lower left sleeve of the tunic. Such badges were awarded for having suffered battle injuries, destroyed enemy tanks or aircraft, sniping successes and the like.

Because of the great diversity of units that were attached to GD, it is impossible to describe in detail each one of the uniform styles. However, among the infantrymen there were some standard features. The most distinctive part of *Grossdeutschland* insignia was a cuff band, worn on the right arm below the elbow, in contrast to the SS formations which wore their cuffbands on the left.

Upon its redesignation as a regiment in 1937 the main source unit, the Wachtruppe Berlin, was issued with a Gothic style 'W' patch that was worn on the epaulettes and shoulder patches. When the infantry training battalion at Döberitz, the other source unit, was expanded the same year, its members added a Gothic 'L' to their epaulettes.

In the German Army, the issue of a cuff band traditionally denoted status as an elite unit and in August 1940 a black cuff title bearing the legend '*Inf.-Reg Großdeutschland*' was issued to the unit. Later, in November, the Führer Escort Battalion, which was formed from *Grossdeutschland*, received its own cuff band. GD's own cuff band changed on a number of occasions

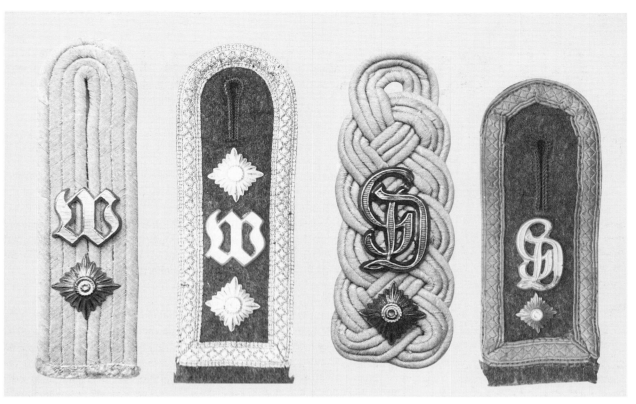

Above: An unnamed Oberleutnant showing the *Grossdeutschland* 'GD' on his shoulder strap and the collar *Litzen* denoting an assault artillery unit.

Right: Eastern Front action from the pages of *Signal*, the Wehrmacht's magazine that was published fortnightly from April 1940 to March 1945.

during the war. Thus, in October 1940 its colour as changed to green, and the legend was simplified to '*Großdeutschland*'. Subsequently, although the legend remained the same, the style and size of the type was changed another four times.

The Führer-Begleit-Battaillon, formed from the ranks of the regiment, was issued on 15 January with an extra cuffband, inscribed with the legend in Gothic German type 'Führer-Hauptquartier' (headquarters) to be worn below the GD band.

UNIFORMS

There now follows a description of what a typical soldier of the Panzer-Füsilier-Regiment would have worn during the 1944–45 period, and a description of the Sturmartillerie uniform from the same period.

The Panzer-Füsilier of 1944–45 would typically be dressed in one of two uniform styles. The first was the standard German Army M43 Tunic with M42 or M43 trousers. The second would be the assault artillery (Sturmartillerie) uniform. This uniform was issued to GD's SPW mounted battalions in 1944.

The M43 Uniform

The M43 uniform tunic was a rationalisation of the M36 design, which had a plain collar, flat, unpleated, unpointed chest pockets and unpointed bellows skirt pockets. At the beginning of the war this was made predominantly from wool, but cellulose was increasingly used over the war years, and as a result the M43 was more cellulose than wool. The lining was made from rayon. As a result of this degradation in fabric quality the tunic now had to be fastened with six buttons. In addition to displaying the *Litzen* (the collar patches that identified rank and arm of service), the collar could also display the dull grey non-commissioned officer's *Tresse* (braid) worn by holders of ranks from Unteroffizier to Hauptfeldwebel. The national emblem of an eagle clutching a Swastika was placed above the right breast pocket, and the divisional cuff band sewn 19cm above the cuff on the right sleeve. The field-grey shoulder straps were piped in white, and the shoulder strap was embroidered with the famous entwined GD monogram. Senior NCOs and officers wore metal versions of this emblem in grey and gilt metal respectively. NCOs' shoulder straps were also edged with the *Tresse* mentioned earlier.

The Sturmartillerie Uniform

In 1944 the armoured battalions of the *Grossdeutschland* infantry regiments (1. Battaillon Panzer-Grenadier-Regiment GD and 1. Battaillon, Panzer-Füsilier-Regiment GD) were issued the Sturmartillerie uniform (though only the first battalions of the motorised infantry regiments were equipped with SPWs). The Sturmartillerie uniform was the same as the Army's black Panzer uniform but in a field grey cloth. The blouson-style jacket was cut at the waist and fastened with a row of buttons arranged vertically on the right hand side. The collar was large and worn open but could be fastened at the neck with a hook and eye. The trousers were tapered toward the ankles giving a bloused effect over the top of the boot. The trousers had an integral belt and front pockets with pocket flaps. The standard GD insignia were worn on this uniform, although the collar Litzen was a standard Litzen over a lozenge shaped patch of field grey wool piped in white, the infantry Waffenfarbe. Officers wore their normal collar insignia attached directly to the collar. Standard white piped shoulder boards were worn with this uniform.

Underclothes

Under the tunic the Panzer fusilier would wear a shirt of either a grey jersey material, or a green or grey cotton, with and without pockets, grey woollen socks or the German copy of the Russian footwraps. Those with experience of conditions on the Eastern Front usually wore footwraps, for extra warmth.

Footwear

Early pictures of *Grossdeutschland* show the troops shod in the familiar German marching boot, but by 1944-45 leather shortages meant that the boot been much reduced in height, and most new recruits were issued with a new style ankle boot. The German Army had trialed the ankle boot in 1935 and re-introduced it in 1942. The style varied according to the manufacturer. Some were all eyeholes, others eyeholes and hooks, some were rough side out on the upper, others were smooth side out all over. In 1944–45 they were supplied in their natural colour, brown.

If they were worn with the M42/M43 trousers, the soldier would probably tuck the ends of the trousers into standard issue gaiters. These were made of heavy canvas and had two buckles and straps to fasten them around the ankles. The gaiters provided some ankle support and also prevented stones and twigs getting into the boots. If worn with the Sturmartillerie uniform then the trousers were probably tucked straight into the boots or into rolled over socks.

In the bitterly cold Russian winters, other types of lined boots found favour with those that could get them.

Headwear

Although, the Panzer-Füsilier in 1944–45 was issued with both the M42 pattern *Stahlhelm* (steel helmet) or the M43 pattern *Einheitsfeldmütze* (field cap), pictures from this period indicate that the latter was more commonly worn.

The M42 helmet was a version of the M35 simplified for quicker production by leaving the rim uncrimped and by casting the ventilation holes directly into the

Below: German infantry move out of their fixed positions during the fighting around Kharkov, 1 June 1942. Note ammunition boxes, MG 34 and other personal equipment.

helmet shell itself. The M43 cap was the standardised field head gear for Army troops, and replaced the previous M38, M40 and M42 pattern caps in production. It was made from field grey wool and featured a long peak, over which the national insignia was stitched. Officers' caps had silver piping to the crown seam, and sometimes this was also placed onto the scallop of the turn up.

In addition the extreme cold of the Russian winter led to a profusion of unofficial fur, fur-trimmed or fur-lined, and wool hats, some of which were donated by the German public after a formal request was made by the Propaganda Ministry.

Other Clothing

Although winter clothing was always in short supply on the Eastern Front, *Grossdeutschland*'s status as an elite unit meant that it got the best of the equipment. It was one of the first units to receive the mouse grey and white (reversible) winter parka issued in the winter of 1942–43, and its men were also issued with numerous other camouflage smocks and snow suits. Another item that was commonly worn over the battledress was the camouflage shelter quarter (see below). Officers overcoats varied greatly from the standard issue field grey type, to the heavy sheepskin-lined item favoured by Generalleutnant Hoernlein.

FIELD EQUIPMENT

Karabiner 98 (K-98)

Introduced in 1898, this rifle (*Gewehr*) was the standard infantry weapon of all German forces. The Kar 98k was introduced in 1935. This weapon, despite plans to replace it with weapons of greater firepower and lower production costs, remained the primary infantry weapon for the entire conflict.

Gewehr/Karabiner 43 (G-43/K-43)

The need for a weapon with greater firepower was recognised early in the war. The unsuccessful G-41, with its complicated muzzle gas cap system was scrapped after delivery of approximately 70,000 rifles, and after examination of captured Russian auto-loaders, the gas system of the Tokarev (SVT40) was incorporated into a new rifle, while retaining the Mauser G-41 extraction system. The new rifle was introduced into service on 30 April 1943. Approximately 350,000 were delivered by 1945.

Maschinen-Pistole 40 (MP-40)

The MP-40 was an improved version of the MP-38 sub-machine gun, intended for use by paratroops and by armoured vehicle crews. It was intended for simple mass construction. Total production was more than a million guns in 1940–44.

Stick Grenade Model 39

The M39 stick grenade was the standard hand grenade of the German Army throughout the war. The grenade consisted of a thin, metal, explosive filled,

Above: 'Only seconds before the attack, a smokescreen already blinds the enemy pocket of resistance. An assault leader glances behind him before launching himself from cover into the open, August 1943.'
So reads the original caption. Certainly the soldier is ready for action; he's left his pack and other weighty equipment behind, has used some foliage to disguise the outline of his helmet and is armed with an MP40 machine-pistol.

cylindrical head that was screwed onto a hollow wooden handle. A friction pull igniter activated the timed fuse when a cord (ending in a porcelain ball) was pulled. The grenade was kept in the 'safe' position by use of a screw off end cap on the wooden handle, which kept the cord and porcelain ball safely in the wooden handle. The fuse time was 4–5 seconds.

Bayonet, Frog and Scabbard
The bayonet frog was used to carry the scabbard on the cartridge belt. It was constructed of leather and came in two styles: mounted and dismounted. The mounted version had a leather tab that would secure the grip of the bayonet to the frog. The bayonet was the final pattern 84/98 Mauser bayonet. The handle was constructed either of wood or Bakelite plastic. The scabbard was made of stamped metal and had a ball on the tip to prevent the scabbard from getting caught on clothing.

Cartridge Belt and Buckle
The leather cartridge belt had a clasp attached to it to be secured at the buckle. The buckle was constructed either of aluminum or steel. The buckle was either unfinished or painted green, with an eagle to denote a Wehrmacht unit.

Cartridge Belt Suspenders
In 1939 testing began on externally worn cartridge belt suspenders. By taking the straps from the Model 1934 field pack and replacing the sewn-on leather pack attachment tabs with D-rings, the external cartridge belt suspenders were created. By late 1940 the new suspenders were in use by the infantry. By 1943 the transition from internal to external suspenders was complete. The suspenders were

Below: Another *Signal* photograph, showing German infantry in 1943. Note colour of uniforms and webbing, and Iron Cross on front man.

produced in two different styles: the dismounted and the mounted. The foot soldier would normally be issued the heavier, dismounted style. The dismounted is identified by the wider shoulder straps, heavier construction, D-ring attachments on the rear of the shoulder harness, and attached lower pack straps which were used for securing the bottom of any attached pack.

Combat Assault Pack
The combat assault pack or A-frame was constructed of a canvas web shaped like an A. This pack was designed to carry essential equipment into action. The A-frame was designed to be used specifically with the dismounted style of leather cartridge-belt suspender. When used, the pack provided places for carrying the shelter quarter, the mess kit, the greatcoat and/or blanket. These items were strapped to the pack with black leather straps.

Model 1938 Gasmask and Canister
The German soldier was issued the Model 1938 gasmask, or GM38. The GM38 was made of synthetic rubber and was fitted with either the FE37, FE41, or FE42 filter elements, which screwed into the snout of the mask. The GM38 had two vision ports. Besides the five elastic straps used to secure the mask to the face, there was a long canvas web strap used to suspend the GM38 around the neck. The fluted metal canister, with a spring loaded lid catch, contained the mask when it was not in use. A small box, on the inside of the lid of the canister, contained two pairs of replacement eyelet covers. A cleaning cloth was also housed in the canister.

Entrenching Tool
The entrenching tool was manufactured in two versions: folding and non-folding. The non-folding type was from a WWI design and had a square blade. The folding tool was designed as a replacement for the older version and began to appear in early 1940. The folding blade was pointed and could be adjusted by means of a Bakelite nut to open at a 90° or 180° angle for digging in. Both versions were stored in carriers suspended from the cartridge belt. The e-tool was also used as a close combat weapon.

Above: The German advance into Russia in 1941 was at such a rate that the infantry were hard-pressed to complete the massive encircling operations. In spite of the 'motorised' nature of the Panzergrenadier, all too often he had to rely on his own two feet to get him into and out of battle. Note the personal equipment—particularly the marching boots: they would be in short supply as the war progressed.

Zeltbahn

The *Zeltbahn* (shelter quarter) or rain poncho, was used both for inclement weather protection and/or camouflage. Made in the shape of a triangle, it had 62 buttons. When four were buttoned together, it produced a 'four-man tent' in pyramid shape, though 'four-man' meant that it was only large enough for three soldiers to squeeze inside; the fourth man was expected to stand sentry duty. The intrepid German soldier found a variety of additional uses for this item. It could be used to form a lean-to shelter or carry a wounded comrade to the aid station, or, as mentioned above, could be an item of clothing. The camouflage pattern seen on the poncho was known as 'splinter' type. See photograph on page 65 for an example of the use of the *Zeltbahn*.

Breadbag Model 1931

The breadbag was carried by every German foot soldier. This satchel was used for carrying a soldier's rations and small personal items: butterdish, fork-spoon, tablet-fuel stove, individual weapon cleaning kit, field cap, dust goggles, extra matches, tobacco, playing cards, etc. The outside of the bag flap could be used for securing the mess tin and canteen.

Below: German grenadiers, wearing greatcoats and carrying rifles, were carried on the back of tanks and self-propelled assault guns towards the enemy.

Mess Kit Model 1931

A mess kit was carried by every German foot soldier. The kit was constructed of two pieces of painted aluminium, which were designed to fit tightly together to form a single container. The lower bowl portion was used for soups and stews, while the upper plate portion was for more solid fare. The mess kit sections, when clamped together, could be used to transport rations for future consumption. Both pieces could be used for cooking, but this quickly destroyed the flat, field-grey or olive drab painted finish.

Canteen and Cup Model 1931

The canteen Model 1931 carried by every German foot soldier, had a capacity of about one litre. The bottle was carried in a brown felt cover that was snapped around it. The drinking cup was made of pressed aluminium, which was painted black and secured to the canteen by a leather strap. The whole canteen was then secured to the breadbag for carrying in the field.

Butterdish

The butterdish or fat container was constructed of Bakelite plastic that was made of two pieces and screwed together. Part of a soldier's daily ration was fat such as butter, margarine or lard. These fats were spread on the bread ration. The butterdish was normally carried in the breadbag.

Soldbuch

The Soldbuch or soldier's pay book was his identity package. This book was on his person at all times. Official entries included a photo i.d. and a record of such things as place of birth, name, equipment numbers, pay records, leave entitlement and so on. Most soldiers also used the Soldbuch to carry money, photos, letters from family, wives, girlfriends, etc.

Identification Disc

As in most armies every foot soldier was issued an i.d. disc, and was required to wear it at all times. The oval zinc i.d. disc was divided in half by perforated slots, and had holes for a cord so that it could be worn about the neck. The information on the disc consisted of the soldier's personnel roster number that was also recorded in his *Soldbuch*, the unit he was assigned to, and his blood type. This was recorded identically on the other half of the disc. In case of death, the disc was broken in half. The portion with the cord stayed on the body for later identification and the other half went to his family with his personal effects.

GROSSDEUTSCHLAND VEHICLE MARKINGS

In September, 1940, during the unit's organisation as a motorised infantry regiment and at the suggestion of the regimental commander Oberst Stockhausen, the familiar white *Stahlhelm* (steel helmet) symbol was chosen to identify regimental vehicles. This remained as the unit insignia for the duration of the war, although it was used in a wide diversity of combinations.

Vehicles carried divisional, tactical, unit and individual markings on the rear. In May 1940 vehicles of the four battalions were distinguished by a square, circle, triangle, or rhombus, over which was painted an identical but smaller shape of contrasting colours, and inside that the divisional Stahlhelm insignia. Command

Above: The battered *Soldbuch* of a German infantryman who served on the Eastern Front.

Below: The white helmet that signifies Grossdeutschland is just visible on the back of this eight-wheeled armoured car. Note frame aerial.

Above: Crew of an Sd Kfz 251 armoured personnel carrier eat from their mess tins without leaving their vehicle. Note the divisional sign of *Grossdeutschland* —the white helmet—painted on the front engine cowling; 14 September 1943.

Below and Right: Two more *Signal* views of *Panzers* in Russia. From 1942 *Grossdeutschland* although it was an infantry division, had tank battalions. By 1944 it was the Army's most powerful infantry unit

vehicles were distinguished by a three-colour pennant, with the 'GD' legend on the white central portion. As additional units were assigned to GD they adopted their own markings. For example, the *Kradschützen* (motorcycle battalion) used a cross bounded by a circle, in addition to the Stahlhelm

Vehicles carried further distinguishing insignia on the front mudguard or the front wing, which in mid-1944 were as follows:

Headquarters (Stab)—GD Pennant on rhombus.

HQ Panzer Regiment—plain square pennant on rhombus.

1st, 2nd, 3rd Battalions Panzer Regiment—plain triangular pennant on rhombus.

HQ Armoured Grenadier Infantry—plain square pennant on SPW symbol.

1st, 2nd, 3rd Armoured Grenadier Infantry battalions—triangular pennant flanked by two circles (to represent wheels of a truck).

HQ Armoured Fusilier Infantry—dark square pennant on SPW symbol.

1st, 2nd, 3rd Armoured Fusilier Infantry battalions—triangular dark pennant flanked by two circles.

Panzer Reconnaissance Detachment (Aufklärungs-Abteilung)—triangular pennant on rhombus masted by smaller pennant.

Flak Abteilung—plain triangular pennant on small circle. Upward pointing arrow on pennant shaft.

HQ Panzer Artillery Regiment—plain square pennant on rhombus. Two vertical lines flank the pennant shaft.

1st Panzer Artillery Regiment—plain triangular pennant on oval. Two vertical lines flank the pennant shaft.

2nd, 3rd, 4th Panzer Artillery Regiments—plain triangular pennant on rhombus. Two vertical lines flank the pennant shaft.

Sturmgeschütz Brigade—plain triangular pennant with border on rhombus. Upward pointing arrow on pennant shaft.

Panzer Engineer Battalion—plain triangular pennant on rhombus. Two upward pointing arrows on top of the pennant shaft.

Panzer Signals Detachment (Nachrichten Abteilung)—plain triangular pennant on rhombus. Single upward pointing arrow on top of the pennant shaft.

Divisions Nachstub Truppe—plain triangular pennant flanked by two circles, two small horizontal lines on pennant shaft.

Replacement Battalion—plain triangular pennant.

PEOPLE

Right: Detachment Commander Major Possl was awarded the Knight's Cross of the Iron Cross in May 1943.

Grossdeutschland's performance in combat and its high press profile ensured that many of its soldiers became household names in wartime Germany. The unit also won a significant numbers of the Ritterkreuz (the Knight's Cross to the Iron Cross) for gallantry. Below are listed the Ritterkreuzträger of the *Grossdeutschland* Panzer Corps, with biographies of some of the most significant personalities.

GROSSDEUTSCHLAND RITTERKREUZTRÄGER

Friedrich Anding
Hans-Dieter Basse
Helmut Beck-Broichitter
Heinz Bergmann
Martin Bielig
Carl-Ludwig Blumenthal
Hans Bock
Georg Bohnk
Max Bohrendt
Heinz Wittchow Brese-Winiary
Wilhelm Czorny
Diddens Diddo
Maxemilian Fabich
Gunther Famula
Franz Fischer
Edmund Francois
Adolf Frankl
Peter Frantz
Eugen Garski
Kurt Gehrke
Alfred Greim
Wilhelm Griesberg
Karl Hanert
Wolfgang Heesemann
Willi Heinrich
Herbert Hensel
Josef Herbst
Hans Hindelang
Walter Hoernlein
Max Holm
Ernst-Albrecht Huckel
Erich Kahsnitz
Franz Kapsreiter
Bernhard Kelmz
Willi Kessel
Rudi Kirsten
Hans Klemm
Heinrich Klemt
Ludwig Kohlhaas
Gerhard Konopka
Gerhard Krieg
Harold Kriegk
Willi Langkiet
Rudolf Larsen
Ernst G. Lehnhoff
Hans Lex
Siegfried Leyck
Karl Lorenz
Heinz Maaz
Helmut Mader
Hanns Magold
Hasso-Eckard Manteuffel
Siegmund Matheja
Leonhard Mollendorf
Oldwig Natzmer
Werner Neumeyer
Heinrich Nuhn
? Paul
Otto Pfau
Fritz Plickat
Wilhelm Pohlmann
Leopold Poschusta
Walther Possl
Josef Rampel
Hans Friedrich Graf zu Rantzau
Adam Reidmuller
Hans Roger
Emil Rossman
Hans Siegfried Graf Rotkirch und Trach
Hans Sachs
Kurt Scheumann
Hugo Schimmel
E. Schmidt
Georg Schnappauf
Hans-Wolfgang Schone
Erich Schroedter
Rudolf Schwarzrock
Clemens Sommer
Ruprecht Sommer
Helmuth Spaeter
Georg Stork
Hyazinth Strachwitz Gross Zauche und Camminetz
Hans Hermann Sturm
Nepomuk Stuzle
Hans Thiessan
Gotfried Tornau
Horst Usedom
Gustav Walle
Horst Warschnaur
Rudolf Watjen
Wilhelm Wegner
Walther Wietersheim

OBERST HEINZ WITTCHOW VON BRESE-WINIARY

Born on 13 January 1914 in Dresden, Brese-Winiary won his Knight's Cross and his Oakleaves to the Knight's Cross while commander of 1./PzGr Regiment 108. He joined GD later in the war, being promoted to Oberst whilst serving with *Grossdeutschland* Panzer Corps.

Brese-Winiary joined the German Army in April 1934 as a member of Infantry Regiment 10 in Dresden and in May 1936 was promoted to the rank of Leutnant. Over the next few years he served as a company officer and battalion signals officer with the 10th Infantry. In May 1939 he was again promoted this time to the rank of Oberleutnant and became a battalion adjutant. On 24 October 1939 he was awarded the Iron Cross 2nd Class. He was awarded the Iron Cross 1st Class on 24 June 1940 whilst serving in France, and on 31 October 1940 he was awarded the Infantry Assault Badge. He then went on to serve in Russia and, as a survivor of the terrible winter of 1941–42, was awarded the Eastern Front Medal. He was also wounded during 1941 while serving in Russia and received the Wound Badge in Black and in December 1941 received the German Cross in Gold.

On 1 March 1942 he was promoted to the rank of Hauptmann and became company commander of the 6th Company IR10. He subsequently served as commander of 2nd Battalion, Panzer-Grenadier-Regiment 108 and 2nd Battalion, Panzer-Grenadier-Regiment 103 and from 14 December 1942 through to 22 February 1943 was commander of Kampfgruppe *Brese*, involved in combat near Stalingrad. During this time he was wounded again and awarded the Wound Badge in both Silver and Gold. In April 1943 he was promoted to the rank of Major and on 15 May 1943 he was awarded the Ritterkreuz. He later on became regimental commander of Panzer-Grenadier-Regiment 108 and fought at the Cherkassy Pocket where he earned the Oakleaves to the Ritterkreuz. He was awarded the Close Combat Clasp on 23 March 1944 and on 1 April 1944 he was promoted to the rank of Oberstleutnant. Finally, on 1 September 1944 he was promoted to Oberst.

As of 3 September 1944 until the end of the war (he surrendered to the Soviets on 18 February 1945) his assignment was commander of Panzer-Füsilier-Regiment *Grossdeutschland* in the *Grossdeutschland* Division.

Brese-Winiary died in 1991.

Below: On 5 April 1943 Hauptmann Magold from the Sturmgeschütz-Abteilung Grossdeutschland received the Knight's Cross of the Iron Cross. During the period from 7 to 18 March 1943, his battery destroyed 26 Soviet tanks and 50 anti-tank weapons around Kharkov.

HERBERT KARL 'HANS' MAGOLD

Born on 16 November 1918, in Unterssfeld, Bad Königshofen im Grabfeld, Bavaria, Magold joined the German Army in 1937 and served in the Polish French and Balkans campaigns. He took part in the invasion of Russia and went on to command 5th Battalion Panzer Regiment 74 in 1942. He was wounded in August 1942 and was sent back to Germany. On his return he commanded 1st Sturmgeschütz Abteilung *Grossdeutschland* in February 1943 in which role he took part in the battles around Kharkov. A short while afterwards during an engagement with Soviet armour he personally accounted for the destruction of five T-34s for which he was awarded the

Ritterkreuz. He was killed in action on 15 September 1944, during the defensive battles at Luzagora near the Dukla Pass in Poland.

HASSO-ECKARD VON MANTEUFFEL

Born on 14 January 1897 in Potsdam, Hasso-Eckard Manteuffel was a career soldier. He joined the Cadet Academy Berlin-Lichterfelde in 1911 at the age of 14 and went on to serve in France with the 3rd Brandenburg Hussar Regiment *Ziethen* as a Leutnant. In October 1916 he transferred with the 5th Squadron to the 6th (Prussian) Infantry Division and at the end of the war was engaged in protecting the Rhine bridges to safeguard the retreat of the field Army. Post-war he served in Freikorps *Oven* in Berlin and was subsequently a squadron commander and adjutant in the 3rd Cavalry Regiment in the 100,000 man Reichswehr. In February 1930 he was promoted Oberleutnant and made chief of the technical squadron of his regiment, and in 1932 was appointed a squadron commander in the 17th Cavalry Regiment. Promoted Hauptmann der Kavallerie in April 1934, in October of that year he transferred to the 2nd Motorcycle Rifle Battalion of the rapidly expanding Wehrmacht and became staff major and training officer of all cadet officers of 2nd Panzer Division 1936–37.

From 25 February 1937 Manteuffel was official adviser to the Inspectorate of Panzer Troops under Guderian at OKH and, subsequently, head of the directing staff at Panzer Troops School II at Berlin-Krampnitz. He was promoted Major in September 1939, Oberstleutnant in July 1941, and Oberst in October 1941, commanding Schützen-Regiment 2 and then 6. On 23 November 1941, during the 7th Panzer Division's final attack towards Moscow Manteuffel's Schützen-Regiment took Klin. By 27 November the area 2½ miles north-west of the bridge at Jakhroma over the Moscow–Volga canal was occupied. Early on 28 November Manteuffel's battle group began an attack in this sector, with the further aim of crossing the canal. They achieved both objectives. On 31 December 1941 Oberst Manteuffel was awarded the Knight's Cross for this operation, to accompany the Iron Cross 1st Class he had won in May 1917.

After being given brief command of Division *Manteuffel* in North Africa (7 February 1943–31 March 1943) he launched a very successful counter-attack in the Tunis area cutting Allied lines. He then led the 7th Panzer Division, being promoted Generalmajor in May 1943 and winning Oakleaves to his Knight's Cross in November that year. He became commander of Panzer-Grenadier-Division *Grossdeutschland* at the end of January 1944, being promoted Generalleutnant.

In 1944 he was awarded Oak Leaves with Swords to the Knight's Cross, before being promoted further in September—to the command of the Fifth Panzer Army as a General der Panzertruppen. This unit won impressive victories during the

Above: On 8 May 1944 a communiqué from the German High Command announced that Generalleutnant von Manteuffel, commander of Panzer Division *Grossdeutschland*, had been awarded the addition of the Oak Leaves with Swords to his Knight's Cross.

Right: Gerhard Konopka, an officer in the *Reichsarbeitedienst* (German Labour Service) and an Oberleutnant der Reserve serving with *Grossdeutschland*, received his Knight's Cross in October 1943. He is seen here wearing his RAD uniform complete with his other military awards (including four *Panzervernichtungsabzeichen* (tank destruction badges) surrounded by admiring young members of the RAD.

Centre right: On 12 November 1942, at the invitation of Dr. Joseph Goebbels, Reichsminister for Propaganda, representatives of the German troops engaged in fighting around Rshev were received in his Berlin ministry. Here he is seen admiring a painting and a captured Cossack sword presented to him by these visiting troops. Standing to his right is Oberleutant Gerhard Konopka and directly behind him Generalleutnant von Hase, Commandant (*Stadtkommandant*) of Berlin.

Below right: Knight's Cross holder, Major Kriegk, commander of the Panzergrenadier Regiment *Grossdeutschland* (wearing bandage), with his adjutant on 14 July 1944.

Below: Hauptmann Hans Lex, Knight's Cross holder and company commander in Panzer Regiment *Grossdeutschland*, 9 October 1943.

Above left: Oberst Lorenz, Commander of the Panzergrenadier Regiment *Grossdeutschland*, offers a drink from his waterbottle to one of his grenadiers, 30 May 1944.

Left: Oberst Graf Strachwitz (right), commander of one of the division's tank regiments, here conferring with one of his tank commanders. Note the stand-off turret armour on the PzKpfw IV behind him.

Above: Oberst Lorenz (wearing cap), commander of Panzergrenadier Regiment *Grossdeutschland*, in conversation with Oberleutnant Konopka. Both are *Ritterkreuzträger*.

Below: The CO of Panzergrenadier Division *Grossdeutschland*, Generalleutnant Hoernlein, in conversation with Oberst Graf Strachwitz (left) on 15 October 1943. Note Strachwitz's cuff title.

Above: Generalmajor Hoernlein standing on his command vehicle observing the effect of a Stuka attack against Soviet positions, August 1942.

Battle of Bulge and almost succeeded in breaking the Allied defence lines. After this battle, Manteuffel became the commander of Third Panzer Army, part of Army Group Weichsel (Vistula), which tried to slow down the Soviet advance on Berlin. On 3 May 1945 he surrendered to the Western allies.

In 1953–57 Manteuffel was a member of the Bundestag and represented the Free Democratic Party. In 1959 he was charged with ordering a 19-year old to be shot for desertion in 1944 and was sentenced to 18 months in prison but was released after serving four months. He died on 24 September 1978 in Reith in Alpbachtal, Austria.

ERNST-OTTO REMER

Born in 1912 Remer was commander of the *Grossdeutschland* Battalion in Berlin at the time of the 20 July 1944 Bomb Plot. Initially he carried out the orders of Oberst Claus Stauffenberg to deploy his *Grossdeutschland* Battalion in and around Berlin's government quarter, but swiftly defected to the side of the regime after speaking to Reich Propaganda Minister Joseph Goebbels and to Hitler personally over the phone who assured him that he had safely survived the plot to assassinate him. Remer was then promoted to the rank of General and given full power to crush the coup and restore order in Berlin.

On the evening of the 20th, Remer accordingly moved his battalion from the government district and ordered his troops to storm the Home Army headquarters to arrest the coup plotters.

Later in the war he became the commander of the Führer-Begleit Division, and survived the destruction of this unit in 1945.

In 1950 he became Deputy Chairman of the neo-Nazi Socialist Reich Party. In this position he delivered scathing attacks on the 'traitors of July 20th' and characterised their legacy as a 'stain on the shield of honour of the German officer corps' who had 'stabbed the German Army in the back.'

In 1952 he was sentenced to three months in prison for 'collective libel against the German Resistance', and fled Germany for Egypt. For the rest of his life he remained a dedicated Nazi, and in October 1992 was arrested in Germany and sentenced to 22 months in prison for publishing neo-Nazi propaganda and denying the existence of the Holocaust. He died in 1997.

DIETRICH VON SAUCKEN

Born in 1892 von Saucken was Panzer-Corps *Grossdeutschland* commander in the final stages of the war, prior to his hurried appointment as commanding officer of the Second Army. He had a varied career in the Wehrmacht, typifying those fortunate to survive six years of war. He had been CO of 2nd Reserve Regiment

1937–40, commanded 4th Schützen-Brigade 1940–41, was general officer commanding 4th Panzer Division 1941–42, commandant Mobile Troops School 1942–43, general officer commanding 4th Panzer Division 1943–44, deputy general officer commanding III Panzer Corps 1944, general officer commanding XXXIX Panzer Corps 1944, general officer commanding Panzer Corps *Grossdeutschland* 1944–45, and general officer commanding Second Army, Eastern Front 1945. He died in 1980.

Below: Carried shoulder high to his assault gun, Hauptmann Frantz, commander of the Assault Artillery Detachment of Infantry Division *Grossdeutschland*, celebrates the award of the Oak Leaves to his Knight's Cross, June 1943.

Commanders of *Grossdeutschland*

Name	CO From	To	Comments
Generalmajor Wilhelm Stockhausen	1/9/39	31/7/41	GD raised as Inf Regt (mot). Stockhausen promoted from Oberst
Generalleutnant Walter Hoernlein	1/8/41	31/1/44	GD becomes Inf Div (mot) 1/4/42. 'Papa' Hoernlein promoted from Oberst
Generalleutnant Hermann Balck	3/4/43	30/6/43	Temporary commander
Generalleutnant Hasso-Eckard von Manteuffel	1/2/44	31/8/44	Promoted to command Fifth Panzer Army
Generalmajor Karl Lorenz	1/9/44	30/11/44	GD becomes Pz Corps
General Dietrich von Saucken	1/12/44	31/1/45	Promoted to command Second Army
General (Pz) Georg Jauer	1/2/45	5/45	Surrendered in various locations
General Willi Langkeit	3/2/45	21/4/45	Commanded Kurmark Division; destroyed by Russians. Langkeit promoted from Oberst
Generalmajor Ernst-Otto Remer	20/7/44	21/4/45	Führer-Begleit-Regiment formed; later (27/1/44) becomes a Brigade; later still (30/1/45) becomes a division. Remer promoted from Oberst, surrendered to Russians

ASSESSMENT

Right: Dr Joseph Goebbels, the Reich Propaganda Minister, was created 'patron' of Panzer Regiment *Grossdeutschland*. He is shown here being greeted by the Regimental Commander with Panzer IIs in the background.

Below right: A battalion commander offers up a light to one of his wounded grenadiers.

It is difficult to assess the effect of an individual unit on a battle, there being so many factors to take into consideration, and well nigh impossible to judge the effect it has on a war, particularly when that unit was on the losing side. When taking account of *Grossdeutschland*'s combat record it is possible to state that the unit did play a decisive role in many of the actions in which it fought and can thereby justly be considered one of the finest infantry formations of World War II.

At the beginning of the war the unit was four battalions strong, and by the end of the conflict *Grossdeutschland* members were fighting in four divisions, in several hastily formed combat groups and other smaller groups. In the early years the process of expanding the unit was a direct result of the Wehrmacht's desire to combat the strength and prestige of the SS, but by 1945 it was a desperate measure to bolster the flagging strength of the army.

In the battle of France, the unit showed for the first time what it was capable of under fire, battling over the Meuse at Sedan to establish a vital bridgehead for the Panzers to sweep through to Channel, and then successfully resisting the Allied counter-attacks on the thin spearhead, despite losing almost a quarter of its strength in the western offensive.

It was if anything stronger for this experience by the opening of the offensive in the east, where it remained for the rest of the war. In the first weeks of the campaign GD was part of the spearhead that made the lightning advance to Smolensk and in the first year of the campaign GD was assigned to many units, often to support assaults on major objectives. By the end of the year it was at the gates of Moscow. In 1942 the regiment was expanded to division size and held the Russian advance at Bolkhov. On the first day of the Caucasus offensive, GD was at the spearhead of an advance that broke through on the Tim. Through the summer it fought at points along the whole line from the Manych River to Rzhev, and was instrumental in the capture of Rostov and the Maikop oilfields.

As it grew in size and stature, so did the expectations of what it could achieve, and during the defensive battles that followed the victories of 1941–42 GD was constantly on the move, transferred from north to south to shore up the weak points in the German lines or else to hold back the tide of the Soviet advance. At Rzhev, from the middle of August 1942 it fought almost continually to hold the city. By the end of a savage year of fighting and despite losing many men, especially first in February and then in December, the unit had grown in stature and never lost its cohesion.

It soon earned the nickname 'The Fire Brigade' because of its almost legendary ability to stamp out crises as they flared up. Nonetheless, the dangerous work of the 'Fire Brigade' took a heavy toll on its men, and increasingly courage alone could

Right: The face of war: festooned with ammunition belts this young grenadier, complete with machine gun and dressed in winter clothing, prepares to move off, April 1943.

not compensate for the overwhelming superiority of the Soviet forces. Again, during 1943, the unit was active across the whole sector of the central and southern fronts, fighting heavy defensive battles and launching counter-attacks. In defence the division proved as skillful as in attack, its desperate defence and heroic counter-attack around Byelgorod in early 1943 being of particular note.

In the thwarted Citadel offensive *Grossdeutschland* was thrown against one of the heaviest and best defended sectors of the Russian line, yet was able to make some local breakthroughs. Around Karachev, in July and August 1943, it thwarted an attempt to encircle the German Eleventh Army with skillful counter-attacks, and at Akhtyrka held up the Soviet steamroller during the retreat, preventing the envelopment of Army Group South. At the Kremenchug bridgehead over the Dnieper in September, it performed heroically again.

1944 was another year of defence, counter-attack and movement, on southern, central and northern fronts. Something of the reputation of the division, and its status among the leadership, can be gleaned from the number of units that carried its name. In the critical battles on the northern front *Grossdeutschland* again distinguished itself, fighting to prevent the Soviet breakthrough to the Baltic and waging a desperate battle to cover the retreat of the German armies through the Memel bridgehead

In 1945, its ranks severely depleted, the corps fought almost to the last man to save Berlin from capture, and its part in delaying the Soviet advance is perhaps part of the reason that Germany was not swamped under the Red tide.

The fact that *Grossdeutschland* was able to survive as a unit during this long period of attrition was in part due to the quality of the officers and men, who were selected from the fittest and ablest recruits. As with all German divisions, *Grossdeutschland* maintained training depots for the reception and integration of replacements instead of sending them piecemeal into the front lines. As the war ground on, combat units were reduced in size and veterans were carefully distributed to form the nucleus for strong primary groups. Strenuous measures were taken to ensure that junior leaders possessed experience and competence; where an American infantry company might boast 150 soldiers and four or five inexperienced lieutenants, a German company might carry 50 or 70 soldiers on its rolls but with a single seasoned officer in command. Importantly, the corps of non-commissioned officers was not diluted to replace officer losses, which might have destroyed the cohesion of the smaller units, and lengthy NCO training courses were continued right up until the end of the war.

Throughout the war *Grossdeutschland* was hamstrung by its own success, which often led to a gross overestimation of its capabilities and propelled it again and again into the fiercest battles. In the closing actions of the war, fighting in disparate units against the Soviet invader, the corps literally fought to the death. Panzer-Grenadier-Division *Grossdeutschland* alone suffered nearly 17,000 casualties. In its short history *Grossdeutschland* tirelessly, professionally and often heroically fought under conditions that would have finished most other military units.

REFERENCE

INTERNET SITES:

http://www.geocities.com/Pentagon/3620/
Achtung Panzer!
Interesting site with very detailed information on German armour.
Great pictures of preserved machines, particularly SPWs.

http://www.feldgrau.com/
This is probably the most comprehensive site currently on the
Web dealing with the German Army before and during World
War II. Well-written and researched, and an intriguing in-
depth interview with a *Grossdeutschland* veteran, too.

http://www.geocities.com/gd7silent/
The group re-enacts the engagements of the 7th Company of
Grossdeutschland. Lots of info, pictures and links to other re-
enactment groups, and still growing. (e-mail:
feldpost@grossdeutschland.com)

http://users.ids.net/~bclauss/index.htm
Homepage of a group of 3. Panzer-Grenadier-Division re-enactors.
Also has links to the 43. Sturm-Pionier re-enactment group.

http://www.angelfire.com/rant/grossdeutschland/home.html
Another US re-enactor site.

http://ourworld.compuserve.com/homepages/hallg/frame1.htm
A Living History UK re-enactment site.

http://www.multimania.com/dday44/uniforme/uniforme.htm
French-language site with some interesting pictures of uniforms,
including a *Grossdeutschland* trooper.

http://www.tankclub.agava.ru/sign/sign.shtml
Russian-language site with excellent illustrations of the tactical
signs of the German Army.

http://www.generals.dk
This is an private project trying to provide biographical data on the army generals of World War II, including many German generals.

http://www.eliteforcesofthethirdreich.com/
Useful information on PKGD and associated units

http://grossdeutschland.freehosting.net/index.htm
This excellent site provides information for game players but has much for the enthusiast including a full examination of vehicle markings at http://grossdeutschland.freehosting.net/vehicle.htm.

BIBLIOGRAPHY

Bender, R. & Odegard, W.; *Panzertruppe—Uniforms, Organisation and History*; Bender, 1980.
Panzer formations 1935–45, Panzer uniforms and insignia, Panzer markings and camouflage are all given in detail.

Culver, B. & Murphy, B.; *Panzer Colours—Vol. 1*.
170 illustrations with 69 full-colour plates provide a detailed account of German armour during WWII.

Delaney, J.; *The Blitzkrieg Campaigns. Germany's 'Lighting War' Strategy in Action*; Arms and Armour, 1996.
Describes the origins of the strategy developed during the interwar years — a strong, co-ordinated, mobile land and air offensive to surprise and envelop an unprepared enemy. Studies how this technique was used during the advances into Poland, Belgium and France then Russia.

Engelmann, Joachim; *German Artillery in World War II 1939-1945*; Schiffer Publishing, 1995. English translation.
This volume of photographs presents a detailed look into the operations, action and everyday life of the Wehrmacht artillery arm.

Erickson, John; *The Road to Stalingrad & The Road to Berlin*; 1983. Weidenfeld and Nicolson/Westview Press, 1983 & 1984
A two-volume definitive study of Stalin's war with Germany.

Efomichenko, Major General; *The Red Army*; Hutchinson, n.d.
Studies the development of The Soviet Army and its exploits from June 1941. Analyses how the Red Army foiled Hitler's plans by pushing back the Axis forces from the Volga and the Caucasus into the Reich itself.

Forty, George, & Duncan, John; *The Fall of France—Disaster in the West 1939–1940*; Guild Publishing, 1990
A pictorial analysis of how the Panzer divisions defeated France within six weeks.

Fuller, J.F.C.; *The Second World War 1939-1945*; Meredith, 1968
This was the first comprehensive strategic and tactical history of the war to be written, and stirred controversy. The book has sixty specially drawn maps and diagrams.

Glantz, David; *From the Don to the Dnieper*;
Illustrations with detailed maps are included in this analysis of Red Army operations — eight vital months of struggle that finally ended Hitler's Blitzkrieg against the USSR.

Grechko, Andrei; *Battle for the Caucasus*;
A Marshal of the Soviet Union pays tribute to his Red Army troops who withstood and repelled the Nazi advance during the battle for the Caucasus, July 1942 – October 1942, a victory that helped change the course of WWII.

Guderian, Heinz; *Panzer Leader*; Michael Joseph, 1952.
The autobiography of the famous German general.

Hoffschmidt, E. J. & Tantum, W. H.; *Combat Weapons, Volume 1 German*; WE Inc, 1968
An illustrated encyclopedia of all German tanks, artillery, small arms, mortars, rockets and grenades.

Jentz, Thomas L.; *Panzertruppen* Vol 1 1933–42, Vol 2 1943–45; Schiffer, 1996
Volume 1 is a complete guide to the creation, organisation and combat employment of Germany's tank force. Volume 2 describes how, when forced on to the defensive, the Panzer formations became expert at counter attacks. The detail is all drawn from original German records.

Kershaw, Robert; *War without Garlands—Operation Barbarossa 1941/42*; Ian Allan Publishing, 2000.
Excellent analysis of the early stages of Germany's war with Russia with plenty of eyewitness accounts.

Kriegsberichter
A bi-monthly magazine for students of the German armed forces in World War II, published in California by Erich Craciun.

Kurowski Franz; *Knights of the Wehrmacht*;
A study of the Knight's Cross holders.

Lucas, James; *Germany's Elite Panzer Force*; Macdonald and Jane's, 1979
A history of the *Grossdeutschland* formation's historic rise from an infantry regiment to a Panzer corps in six years.

Lucas, James; *War on the Eastern Front—The German Soldier in Russia*; Jane's, 1979
An account of the war against the Soviet Union from the German angle.

Lucas, James; T*he Last Year of the German Army May 1944—May 1945*; BCA, 1994
A complete study of structural changes made to try and overcome the army's depletion and an insight into some of its last battles.

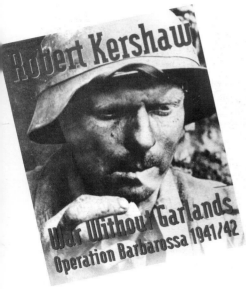

McLean, Donald B. (Ed); *German Infantry Weapons Vol 1*; Normount Armament Co, 1967
Originally published in 1943 to assist Allied commanders, details the design and construction of weapons and their ammunition.

Messenger, Charles; *The Art of Blitzkrieg*; Ian Allan, 1976
Studies Blitzkrieg's evolution as a technique of war and describes how Hitler used the theory so effectively.

Metelmann, Henry; *Through Hell for Hitler*; Patrick Stephens, 1990
A dramatic account of fighting with the Wehrmacht in Russia.

Mitcham, S.A. Jnr.; *Hitler's Legions*; Leo Cooper, 1985
The organisation and technical aspects of the German divisions are described. Every part of the army is covered.

Nafziger, George F.; *The German Order of Battle Panzers and Artillery in World War II*; Greenhill Books, 1999.
Defeinitive orders of battle.

Pallud, Jean Paul; *Blitzkrieg in the West – Then and Now*; After the Battle, 1991
Fully illustrated. Then and now photographs show how Germany, in just sixty days, caused France to capitulate during 1940.

Piekalkiewicz, Janusz; *Operation Citadel*; Presidio, 1987
A complete illustrated analysis of the Battles of Kursk and Orel which shattered Nazi ambitions in Russia.

Sajer, Guy; *The Forgotten Soldier*; Harper and Row, 1971. English translation
A German soldier, drafted into *Grossdeutschland* in 1942 despite being of French/German descent, provides a vivid chronicle of the faceless anonymity of total war in the endless bitter wastes of Russia.

Scheibert, Horst & Culver, Bruce (Ed); *Panzer Grenadier Division Gross Deutschland*; Squadron/Signal, 1987
An excellent pictorial reference work on the *Grossdeutschland* units.

Above: The crew of a *Hornisse* (Hornet) anti-tank gun awaits orders. Designed to carry a 88mm PAK 43/1 on a Panzer III or IV chassis, the Hornisse was introduced into combat in late 1943.

INDEX